10 WAYS TO ACCELERATE YOUR WEALTH

HOW TO ALIGN YOUR FINANCES FOR AN ABUNDANT LIFE

REBECCA ROBERTSON

authors
AND CO.

CONTENTS

WHAT OTHERS FELT ABOUT THE BOOK.

"I loved reading this book. It's not often you get a fabulous financial adviser helping you look at the practicalities of managing money AND deal with the inner games, thoughts and beliefs which challenge us. If you're looking for a practical, step by step way to become financially free, then look no further. I love the exercises and simple ways you can start managing your money and creating greater wealth. A fab read for every woman wanting to take better control of her wealth."

– Yvette Taylor Creator, of EAM – The Energy Alignment Method™

www.yvette-taylor.com

———

"This is a brilliant book, and should be recommended reading for every woman. A mix of personal experience, psychology and education, it's easy (and enjoyable) to read and packed with important financial insights, practical exercises, and wisdom. It delves into your personal relationship with money, and helps you to identify and unpick any bad habits – and develop a healthier, more liberating relationship with money. It's a comprehensive, yet common sense, approach to finance that you'll reap the rewards from for the rest of your life."

– Hannah Martin, co-founder Talented Ladies Club.

www.talentedladiesclub.com

———

"One of the greatest challenges facing women (and men for that matter) is that we are not taught about money. At best, we learn to make it, but rarely to manage or grow our wealth. With practical exercises and simple explanations, this great book goes a long way to overcoming this problem. Her 'back to basics' approach will do financially overwhelmed women and their families the world of good."

-Dr Joanna Martin.

www.oneofmany.co.uk

———

"Whatever your money situation right now, this book holds precious gems and long-awaited answers to your money questions. Rebecca Robertson is on a mission to empower women when it comes to money - equipping them with the essential information, understanding and tools to improve financial health, build financial wealth and ultimately create the sort of financial security and freedom that is life changing.

Whatever your own financial goals and aspirations, developing your financial health and wealth with the sort of insights and know-how contained in this book is an important element of becoming fully empowered."

-Nicola Huelin, founder of Mpower Mastermind Groups for Mums in Business.

www.mpower.global

———

INTRODUCTION

HOW TO CREATE AN ALIGNED FINANCIAL PLAN FOR AN ABUNDANT LIFE.

Are you feeling out of control with your money?

Knowing that there are a million things on the to-do list but not knowing where to start is really overwhelming.

That feeling is normal for everyone from all walks of life, from women in high management, running businesses, working part time or a full-time mother.

We all have the same worries:

What happens to my kids if anything happens to me?

What is the impact if I stop having an income?

How can I cut back on spending without reducing the rewards?

How can I ensure I can have more security and worry less about the future?

Imagine if we could create ***an aligned financial plan for an abundant life.*** What would that look like for you, or your family, or society as a whole?

Would we see families from all walks of life holding onto money and passing it down the generations more, creating a legacy, reaching the grandchildren?

Would we see more women choosing to work differently, not doing jobs they hate?

Would we see more women retiring earlier or leaving relationships they don't like, taking longer maternity leave or having more children?

Would we see women spending their money differently, changing markets and society with the power of spending?

Would we see more women giving to charity and starting to change the world?

Would we see more ethical investments, therefore more ethical businesses invested in?

I believe we would.

What is Female Financial Independence?

This is where a woman can walk out of her job without having to worry about paying the bills – of course, this applies to men as well. Naturally, women worry if they will be employed elsewhere at the same level of income.

This is where a self-employed woman or business owner finds themselves able to take some time out without worrying over being able to afford to continue to pay themselves. Often, women with young children find themselves working late just to keep their business going, let alone taking time off.

This is where you can walk out of a marriage or long-term, financially committed relationship and not be fearful that you will be unable to keep the roof over your head, which for women is their biggest concern, especially if they have children or have taken a step back from their career to support a partner.

This is where, though you might be in a full-time career and have children, your partner and yourself have made financial decisions jointly and you still have money to spend without having to ask permission.

This is where you get to choose to take time out to look after your elderly parents if necessary, or you can pay for a career yourself if they don't have the ability.

This is where you get to choose when to stop work, or slow down, not based on whether your partner stops or even has to work longer hours than they currently do.

Female Financial Independence should be our top priority. We must lead our daughters and our granddaughters to believe that there is a different way and that we do not just accept the way things were done many years ago.

I wrote this original copy in 2016. Five years later and the percentages have moved a few points in the right direction. But the major shift is that more women are saving. Scottish Widows' Women & Retirement 2020 report[1] states that 59% of women aged over 30 are saving adequately - at least 12% of their income. This is the highest figure from the respected life insurance and pension group's annual insight, which started in 2005. However, the pension gap is still there between men and women, with 54% of men investing compared to 46% of women. And that does not take into account the amounts invested, as women are generally paid less, and are more likely to have gaps in employment and work part time. Scottish Widows found that the difference was £100,000 invested in pensions over a 44-year career, meaning men had more money in the piggy bank to live off of in retirement.

But seven out of 10 people aged over 90 are women. Yes, women tend to live longer, therefore we have even more reason to make sure that more funds are available.

I am happily married to a man. We have been together for 21 years and have two children together. I was made redundant at the height of my career when I was pregnant and earning more than my husband. I have started a business and gone through all the highs and lows you expect as an owner. I was brought up by my father, a single parent. We were council tenants but had just what we needed because he worked all the hours to make sure he could provide for the family. This meant I had to be looked after a lot of the time by my grandparents, but it also meant I had tremendous respect for men. Both my husband and my father are my rocks and have helped me to get to where I am today. This is not about the exclusion of men but about equality - for women to have the same financial power as men.

Working in a male dominated industry for many years, I was trained by managers who were men, compliance checked by male supervisors and monitored by male managers. Without knowing, I mimicked their mannerisms and their way of doing things. I became, like a lot of women in the industry, institu-tionalised. I was often the only female adviser and certainly the only female manager with adviser experience. The women in the office were administrators. The environment did not encourage them or new starters to progress. The industry has a reputation for being pushy and at times selling to clients, not always putting them first, which I have experienced. Many women do not feel comfortable working in this kind of environment and they are not encouraged to progress either. Consequently, 85% of financial planner/mortgage brokers are men. I do not include bank staff as they are tied agents and, unless they get established in an independent firm before they have a family, the opportunity becomes less likely.

For these reasons, I believe women have not felt they can trust the industry as a whole to get independent advice. Research has revealed that women are less likely than men to seek professional financial advice across all areas of finances, with only 36% of women taking professional advice to help them plan for retirement compared to 46% of men[2]. Some 45% of women say communication from providers is "complicated and incomprehensible"[3]. Some 79% feel that we do not have the right level of information or the knowledge about investments products. This figure is highest, at 87%, for the youngest group of women we surveyed.

Imagine if schools provided financial education and then families, particularly women, followed it up with home education. Would students get into less debt? Would those in their mid-twenties make different financial decisions? I believe so.

Women in the past have tended to rely on their partners to deal with the financial decisions. It was not until 1975 women in Britain were allowed to open their own bank account. But we are finding more couples are making decisions together, or the female is holding the purse strings and therefore, wanting to make educated financial decisions. Women have every reason to make sure their financial future is secure. They tend to have gaps in employment after looking after their children, meaning many will have a reduced pensionable income. But, generally speaking, women are living longer and surviving their partners, they often have jobs that are based on their passion not how much they earn, they are more generous in nature (not putting their financial needs first but their family's wants) and, they are less likely to take risks with their money.

Apparently by 2025, women are poised to take control of the bulk of Britain's wealth, according to a report from the Centre for Economics and Business Research[4].

It said women currently own 48% of the UK's personal assets but this would rise to 60% by 2025 as women reap the dividend of better qualifications, more equal pay, higher levels of home ownership and that longer life expectancy.

That report was written in 2005. We have seen the shifts but, as a society, are we really as far ahead as we would expect?

In this book I am going to share 10 ways to accelerate your wealth. I hope that by the end you will have the confidence and knowledge to know exactly what you need to do to clear debt, earn more money, manage your money, save, plan and invest.

The first step in this process is our mindset, where we have come from and where we want to get to. Our past does not dictate our future, however, when it comes to money, past experiences can certainly establish our expectations, our goals and the focus we give to it.

We will be exploring what could be holding you back from taking the actions needed to put the things in place to create this abundant life as well as taking the practical steps needed, which anyone from any background can do. This is for you. This is for everyone... from any walk of life.

Coming from humble beginnings myself and seeing the impact of what financial education, knowledge and being aligned with your finances has had on hundreds of clients and thousands of women over my 21 years in the industry, I know that being in control of your finances brings a level of confidence and a feeling of strength that is incredible.

My passion, for over 10 years of running my own business, has been, and will continue to be, to support women to achieve financial success – whatever that looks like to them. I have seen too many clients and family members in relationships and jobs they do not want to be in, living a life that makes them feel as if they are not receiving the best possible rewards.

I want you to have confidence, to be able to make strong educated decisions and to live your life on your terms.

As a qualified, FCA-registered Director and Independent Financial Adviser, the information I provide in this book is information only. I am sharing general knowledge of financial matters. For independent bespoke advice, you should seek out an adviser who suits your requirements. You can check out my podcast for more on this subject.

Rest assured my passion to support your shift is a massive one and I feel certain that the content of this book will empower you with your finances now and again in the future, no matter what stage you are at.

Much Love

Rebecca

WHY WOMEN BEHAVE DIFFERENTLY WITH MONEY TO MEN

A survey carried out by the Chartered Insurance Institute (CII) found that women say they do not understand some financial products enough to put their hard-earned cash towards them. As a result, they feel less confident about making financial decisions than men do. Women have so far tended to place their money into products such as current accounts or cash ISAs (individual savings account) instead of the more complex investment plans usually chosen by men.

Why is there this lack of understanding?

History tells us that women have taken the back seat when it comes to family finances. The Married Women's Property Acts 1870 gradually, over a period of 23 years, gave women the rights to own assets independently.

But it seems women have taken time to realise the fact that they need to know just as much as men about the family finances. More and more women are finding out that they do not know what to do when their spouse passes away and have been the subject of unlawful or incorrect advice, struggling to determine what is right or wrong.

The media have often stated that this is down to women not being interested in finance because it is boring and worrying, but do we really believe this?

Current financial offerings are marketed as products, with a lot of jargon associated with them. This does not attract women, who want to know exactly what they are buying, in plain English, from a person they can relate to so they can put a frame of reference around it.

I often hear clients saying they have got advice elsewhere already but felt the process was rushed, that things were not explained carefully and that they did not feel they could ask questions.

Looking inside their heads.

Money is a very emotionally loaded discussion and it drives more couples apart than other issues. Psychotherapist Olivia Mellon has done much research into this topic and has come up with some useful insights.

She mentions that money is inextricably linked with power, happiness, security, control, dependency, independence, freedom and love. So, if someone has an issue with money, to talk about it brings up an awful lot of other problems that have been stored in their subconscious. This can evoke some deep-seated emotions. To talk about money in a relationship can bring about guilt and anxiety, which can prevent such conversations taking place. But the problems do not go away and can often become worse.

Olivia Mellon says that men are brought up to see the world as competitive and hierarchical, there is always someone above you and someone below, however women see the world as co-operative and democratic, therefore sharing. Women are also encouraged to be seen as needy and vulnerable while men are discouraged from such behaviour.

When seeing clients, there are usually two roles taken by men, either "I'll pretend I am listening although I know this is important but 'she' (partner) can deal with this" or "I'll have a final say on this, I need to make sure I am protecting my family". However, in reality, if the partner has strong enough opinions then the man is often swayed towards her way of thinking.

This is different from when I first started my career, more than 15 years ago, where I was either speaking to the male or the female, often the male. Women have taken over making financial decisions around the household bills and food shopping due to procedures nowadays. In 65% of households, in fact, women are making those financial decisions. Men have, therefore, started to step away from the day-to-day decisions. Unfortunately, it has meant that some families have not then received financial advice, which is not on a comparison website. The new age of the female financial consumer is still evolving, she is independent and wants to understand the full spectrum of advice and make an informed decision.

So why are female financial advisers a good idea?

In research, women have stated they are put off from dealing with financial advisers because of the jargon that is put out in the media and negative stories that friends, family and the press have put forward. So, they miss out on potentially crucial information that could improve their financial situation.

There are many women who prefer to deal with a female financial adviser as they are discussing personal details because all finance is always linked to lifestyle choices and family situations.

Unfortunately, as a high percentage of advisers are men, it has given clients the impression that some of them do not have the client's best interest at heart. There are some amazing male advisers in the industry, who do not deserve this judgment. But the impression has already been made. The client wants to be listened to and be confident that they are not going to be made to feel ridiculed or incompetent in some way. Female advisers will often give an impression of caring and nurturing clients, wanting to listen to their needs and allowing clients the time to make decisions without pressure.

So why bother?

Women, in general, have more commitments and challenges within their lives than ever before. They tend to be the gender that juggles with parents, children, households and jobs/businesses. It's not surprising that they actually do need different financial advice than men. It is also vital that they see finance as an important part of their lives and something that they need to know and understand fully.

After all, as we have already discussed, women tend to live longer than men, so need to provide for themselves for longer. They also earn less than men over a lifetime because of career breaks to have children, taking part-time jobs, or caring for elderly parents.

As mentioned in the introduction, the Centre for Economics and Business Research predicts that by 2025 women will own 60% of the nation's personal wealth. The study, carried out for the Liverpool Victoria Friendly Society, found there were already 47,355 female millionaires aged between 18 and 44, compared with 37,935 men[1].

Women are achieving better qualifications than men at GCSE and A-level. More women than men go on to higher and further education.

When women move into employment, they still encounter gender discrimination. Gross hourly earnings are 83% of the male average, though this does compare to 63% in 1970.

Liverpool Victoria said: "Given the increasing levels of education, success amongst women – coupled with the changes in mix of professions – this is expected to rise to at least 90% by 2025."

Nearly two-thirds of women aged 20 to 24 live away from their parents, compared with 44% of men. Single women are more likely than single men to own their own home and are well placed to benefit from increasing property prices. Women who marry are likely to outlive their husbands, so wives are more likely to inherit their husbands' wealth than vice versa. Women live, on average, until 81, while male life expectancy is 76.6 years.

Liverpool Victoria also said: "This change will come about due to the rise of a cohort of financially sophisticated younger women, adding to the traditional sources of female wealth, such as marriage and inheritance."

But women are less likely than men to make long-term financial plans or start a pension. The Friendly Society said single women were much less likely to have mortgage protection, employment protection or permanent health insurance.

I am seeing more higher-earning career women making more empowered decisions every year, but the progress is slow and I wonder what can be done to speed up this evolution.

Our history and personal stories will give many of us the answers to that, we all have a story to tell and how that sets us up for success or failure.

2

MY MONEY STORY, PART 1

The purpose of writing this book at the outset was purely to help more clients and to be able to support existing clients with more information around money management and creating wealth. As with most situations, it did not stay this way. As time went by, more people encouraged me to write my own story. Because it was my own money story, which was just as important as my original message, I fought this for quite some time, saying it was not about me, it was about the clients I was helping. This was not the 'Becky show'. I loved my business and what the brand stood for, but I hid behind it, as most women do. We step back and do not push ourselves into roles or positions that would be beneficial to us. We accept where we are, believing that's where we deserve to be. Even when we are encouraged and supported to make a leap, we still step back and do not feel as if we deserve or are worthy of the role/position. Why? What is it in our make-up that we can't see it for ourselves? I know women who have the full ability and potential but virtually sabotage themselves along the way, just to prove that they were right in the first place. We deserve more.

We should demand more. Why not? We all have the right and the skill to achieve whatever we wish. We just have to believe it and grasp it with both hands.

Of course, there is the other side to the coin where the women who do this are seen as money-grabbing or a "bitch". It might be the green-eyed monster but I also feel that the way women are portrayed in films and cartoons does have an influencing factor. Take Cruella de Vil. She has money, drives a flash fast car and has a large house – but she is the villain. Women are portrayed as either the businesswomen with no children and, therefore, so career-minded that there is no time for anything else in her life, or the mother figure at home who cooks fresh meals every day and waves her children off at the school gates. We are so much more than either of these versions. If either were to become successful in their own right, often the individual would be considered a hard-nose person with no emotion in the decision making – just as men are expected to be strong, make business-like decisions and have no emotion in their conviction. It is time we, male and female alike, let go of these stereotypes and stand in the space we believe belongs to us, while showing others they can do the same.

So, I have sat here nervously writing out my thoughts in the hope it will help others and with the belief in my heart that I deserve my spotlight as much as the next person. Is it because I am a millionaire, or that I have a perfect life, or that I know everything and could not learn anymore? No, none of these things. If we all waited until we were in the perfect position, no one would achieve anything. We would just see others flying ahead of us and we would be left wondering when it is our time.

It often surprises people who know me that I was brought up by my dad, a single parent. They hear me speak about women's challenges, how women need more support and encouragement. In fact, I was raised in a male environment, my dad being a real man's man. My passion for the female cause, comes from my own experiences and those of the tribe of women I have around me. I see many more women needing financial assistance and less sure of where to start or turn. My female focus comes from my feeling that we have not even seen the start of what we can achieve.

My father was always a strong character and force in my childhood. He comes from a generation where you work hard, pay your bills and go to the pub on a Friday after work. As an industrial engineer, he got his hands dirty and worked long hours. His dad was in the Second World War and worked in the mines and his mum worked in a sewing machine factory - that was the true British working class. He saw those in high-level roles as people who went to university and were born with a silver spoon in their mouth. From his view point, there were limits; you could not be anything you wanted. You couldn't live the life of your dreams. He encouraged me to work hard, do my best and maybe I would get my own house with a mortgage and have a good job to pay the bills. His advice has actually done me well and given me a strong work ethic, I love and respect him very much. But for a long time, I believed that we all had limits and that high levels of wealth were only for those from another social status. I certainly could not own a horse and send my children to private school.

At primary school, I wasn't classed as an academic. Who was I to disagree? I sat next to people who would help me maybe more than they should. Looking at my own strong-willed daughter now, I probably did not help myself much. My

memories of homework or learning from home was my nan
trying to do spellings with me and getting frustrated with me,
likewise my dad helping me with fractions. I just did not get it.
There were little expectations for me to aspire to be something
or someone. When it came to going to secondary school, they
considered holding me back for a year, allowing me time to
catch up. They decided to keep me with my friends, and
emotionally that was the best thing for me.

When starting secondary school, they did not know what do
with me. I didn't have any special needs but I wasn't main
stream. At that time, a few years ago now, they did not have
special schools for children. So, they placed all those pupils who
were below the bar into one class. As I sat in that room, I
remember looking around wondering what I had done to
deserve to be there. The work they gave me was too easy and I
knew that I needed to work harder to get ahead and back to the
classes with my friends. It was the first moment in my life when
I knew that I deserved better and that I was the only one who
would make it happen. After a year, I was up in main stream
and in English I was in the high set. With maths, however, I was
still playing catch up.

When it came to choosing careers, I wanted to be a vet. The
careers' teacher looked at me and suggested maybe becoming a
hairdresser. I was the least 'girly' person ever. Brought up by my
dad, older grandparents and having an older brother, I was a
tom-boy. When out playing with friends, all boys, I was picked
to play football third or fourth, not last. I was one of the lads.
My dad being a single parent with a family of five to support
(including my grandparents) he didn't take me clothes shopping
but instead, I wore my brother's old tracksuits.

Once, my mum bought me a pair of the latest Reebok trainers with an air bubble for my birthday. I wore them into the ground. Something my dad would never be able to afford or buy. This was one of my first financial lessons. My mum was married to someone who worked within local government in a senior role. They had a large cottage in a pretty village and shopped in John Lewis and Marks & Spencer, whereas I lived in an ex-council property and there was little spare money for any extravagances. It was two different worlds. This is where I learned that you had to make do with what you had and you would never afford to have nice things; it was extravagant and unnecessary. My first money block.

So back to my career choice. My family did not think being a hairdresser was the right choice, either. However, they explained becoming a vet meant having to acquire several GCSE's, five or more A-Levels before six years-plus at university. They did not believe it would be right for me or that I would be able to achieve it. After this, I didn't know what I wanted to do. I took my GCSE's achieving a few, nothing to be that proud of. A very similar story to other people's experiences.

At 15, I left school and the only job I could do was strawberry picking. I got on my bike and rode it out to the fields, several miles away from home. I think I ate more strawberries than I picked in the first few weeks. Starting college at 16, to pay for my train fare I worked in KFC and in factories, fruit packing until midnight. I resented the fact that my family did not pay for me, but this was my second financial lesson: only I could obtain money and no one was going to give it to me. But this has blocked me to think that to earn money, we have to work hard for it, it will not just come to us.

Fast forward a couple of years, I had gained a NVQ in Business at college and started working in office junior-type roles. The first was as a filing clerk for a distribution company where I had thousands of pink and yellow slips to place in 30 cabinets - beyond boring. At 19, I was made redundant from a long-standing receptionist role. I found myself working in the Job Centre as a temp, helping others to find employment. Well, those who were interested. After three months, I was on my last working day, a Friday, thinking I would be signing on myself on the Monday. I had a phone call from an agency asking if I wanted a job the following day. What office is open on a Saturday, I thought. I told them my days of working in factories and KFC were over. They explained that it was working in a bank. My little head could not imagine me working in a bank. That was for those who went to university and were clever with maths. I had only just got my dad to open a bank account for me. I knew nothing about finances or money.

The next day, I went to work and saw a queue outside the bank at 8:30am. Getting in the building, I was taken downstairs to the staff kitchen area where on the table were hundreds of leaflets. They contained details of all kinds of 'terms and conditions' and types of accounts. I did not know the difference between an easy-saver and a bond... or what an overdraft was. Within half an hour, a group of us were up on the bank counter. I opened the draw of the desk and there sat thousands of pounds in cash. I had never seen or imagined so much money before. The doors of the bank opened and people came in filling up. Now, this lack of training would not happen in this day and age. The branch was so short staffed, all the team on that Saturday were temps, apart from a manager. I had never handled more than £200 cash before, let alone counting through large wads of notes in front of strangers. I was so nervous.

Who in their right mind would want me working for them in a bank? I had few qualifications for it and didn't even understand what a bank did. The thing was though, I was actually really good at it. The counting got easier with practice and I loved chatting to new people on the counter. Within three months, I was head cashier and was taken on permanently. This was the start of my financial services career.

The two money blocks I've mentioned went on to live with me for another 20 years. Only once I had worked out they existed, and then how I could remove them, was I able to step up and take the shifts I needed and deserved.

3

MONEY BLOCKS

Why do we have blocks about money?

Most research states that money blocks stem from our early days. Maybe a parent has said that "money is the root of all evil" and that "being rich is selfish". These beliefs can be instilled in you without you even being aware, and then throughout your life, you find yourself being without money because of an unconscious fear of having it.

A lot of financial advisers tell you that in order to be prosperous you need to make sure that you own your own home, pay off your debts, keep savings and, if you want to be a millionaire, run your own business. However, as much as we read this, many people have no luck at making their millions and instead waste money on get-rich-quick schemes or the lottery without success. So, why is that?

As I said before, it could be a belief that has been passed to you by your parents. You are holding this as your own belief and using it to confirm that what you believe is correct when you are actually holding a losing ticket every week.

How do we break down those blocks?

Becoming aware of our beliefs about money is a start. Breaking the connection between your parents' money blocks and your own is also necessary. Try to find out what these blocks are... because once you do, you will be in a better position to consciously change your beliefs around money to more positive ones such as, "there is more than enough money to go around" or "I can enjoy money and still save for the future at the same time".

Here are some crucial questions to ask yourself to find out your innermost beliefs around money. You can also do this exercise with a personal friend or a business friend:

What is your most painful money memory?

What is your most joyful money memory?

How did these experiences shape how you use money now?

What three things did your parents teach you about money?

When growing up, was your family, rich, poor or middle class?

What were your family's values around money?

What is your greatest financial fear?

What are your most important financial goals?

What are you willing to do differently around money?

Beliefs and ideas about money can also be attributed to personality. There are many different traits and these can be directly linked to a person's attitude towards money.

What does our personality contribute to our beliefs about money?

There has been a large scientific study carried out in the UK to find out about personality traits and how they affect a person's relationship with money. It gives a simple yet effective explanation about our relationship with money for the vast majority of us.

The research was called the BBC's Big Money Test, which was a survey conducted on more than 100,000 people in 2015 by Professor Adrian Furnham, from University College London, Professor Mark Fenton-O'Creevy, from the Open University, and BBC Lab UK. Its aim was to find out how personality affected attitudes to money and how relationships with money impacted the risk of going into debt.

Firstly, the research established that there are four distinct ways people view money. These have been labelled as Status Spender; Generous Indulger; Secure Saver; and Independence Lover. I will explain each of these shortly.

It determined that our relationship with money can, and does, affect the risk of being in trouble financially. Depending on which personality type you fall into can affect the risk level of getting into debt. There were other factors that affected our relationship with money:

- A person's age was a big factor. It seems that young adults were at the bottom of the pile when looking at money management, mainly because they were not thinking about the future.
- Gender is also important to mention because women and men in general see money in a very different way. Women are more likely to spend more, yet were more

worried about how much they were spending than men. Men were more likely to see money as their route to freedom or as an achievement of their goals. Studies have also shown that women, in general, donate more to charity and will give money to their children before spending it on themselves.

The study then revealed that there are times when we are susceptible to thinking about money in wasteful ways... such as worrying all the time about how much we are spending, denying that we buy unnecessary things, and retail therapy - the buying of things to make us feel better.

So, going back to the four ways people view money and how it affects their spending, here is a summary of each:

Status Spender

Money means power to these people and they will usually be the type of people who will have the latest gadgets or drive the flashiest cars and will most likely buy everyone a drink in the pub or buy their friends dinner. These people are the most likely to have problems with personal relationships and could end up with large financial debt.

These types of clients will be approaching us about clearing debts and how they can get their head above water. No matter how often they have achieved this, they have not looked at why they have been spending in this way nor what has made them feel that they need these 'status' items.

Generous Indulger

These people love to buy gifts for their family and friends. They enjoy giving to the extent that it replaces genuine affection, according to psychologists, and they can have difficulty with their children as they get older because their children expect gifts all the time and more money to be spent on them at every opportunity.

I see a lot of women with children lavishly spending fortunes on their new babies, enough clothes for an African village, and their spending gets out of control; it makes them feel like they are taking care of their child better by purchasing these items. Often, I see their partner concerned about their spending and not understanding why they feel the need to do it. Once that habit has started, it is hard to change. It can extend into the children as they become older with the endless list of toys and higher end clothes, etc.

Secure Saver

Money is security to these people and they feel better when they put it in the bank or into some kind of savings, even when they don't need to save it. These people can end up denying themselves and their loved ones opportunities that could improve their financial situation because they are unwilling to take the risk.

I met a lady who had £35,000 sitting in an ISA, she kept the money separate from her family's monthly outgoings and savings and took great comfort that the money was there in case of emergency. To her, the idea of moving it or touching it was crazy.

INDEPENDENCE LOVER

Getting away from it all with holidays or taking sabbaticals are what these people crave. They use money to break free from the burden of everyday life. The important thing for this type to remember is that they need to look at other financial aspects of life, such as preparing for the unexpected events, for example ill health.

I have a client who really doesn't care how much she spends - not on little things, but holidays and summer holidays... and she will re-mortgage and take equity out her house to facilitate this. Her belief is that life is short after all, and the money is there to spend.

So, which one are you? Where do you sit within these habits?

What would you need to change in your spending to create financial abundance?

And here is your first of 10 ways to accelerate your wealth –

Number 1:

Understand your money story and how it is showing up in your spending, finances and the ways you are reacting to money.

Grab a note pad and write down all the questions I listed at the start of this chapter.

The first two questions: What is your most painful money memory? What is your most joyful money memory?

Draw a line on your pad, this is your time line. From birth to now. Above the line is positive and below the line is negative.

Plot out milestones in your life, like starting school, put a dot and your age. Continue down the line, adding secondary school, first job, leaving home or buying your first car, etc. Once you have finished, go back and consider the two questions above. Plot any negative or positive memories. Using the pad write out those memories and consider how they might be playing out in your life to this day?

One really simple way to change what stands in the way of you and more money is a technique call The Energy Alignment Method (EAM) ®.

EAM is a powerful personal development tool. Designed to enable you to quickly change your thoughts, beliefs, memories, patterns, emotions and behaviours so you can feel more positive, happier and in flow (about anything it works on so much more than money).

It is all too common for people to experience feelings of stress, anxiety, worry, overwhelm and uncertainty when they think about money. The truth is focusing on money in this way only brings more negativity, which is usually creates the exact opposite of the thing you want! Which is of course more money in your life.

Many personal development and law of attraction methods talk about having a positive mind set, doing meditations and affirmations. Whilst this IS essential, there is often one thing missing. How do you ACTUALLY let go of the things in your way? Those thoughts, doubts, beliefs and bad past experiences.

With EAM we address both, with 5 simple steps you can transform what is standing in your way. This means you feel happier, more confident and able to think more positively about anything which is troubling you.

THE 5 Steps to EAM

The process works by tuning into what is happening in your energy. You can do this by using a method from Applied Kinesiology known as "the sway'. This process is a muscle and energy testing technique which gives us an Ideomotor, or subconscious response. Which put simply is a YES or NO reaction from your body in answer to a question?

Before you begin (and when you're using this for the first time) we need to ensure that your YES and your NO are the right way around.

Stand with your feet hips width apart and relax your knees and your hips. Close your eyes.

Check you are aligned by saying something like "My name is (Say your name)" and notice if your body gentle sways forwards or backwards. You can check this with other simple question like "my date of birth is …." Or "My middle name is …." Etc. usually your sway forwards is a YES and backwards is a NO, sometimes it can be something else, but that takes more explanation. Now you know your YES and your NO – you can ask your body simple yes/ no questions.

Think about something which may have been troubling you. Stand with your feet hips width apart, close your eyes and relax your knees.

The Five Steps of EAM – One Page Guide

Here's a simple quick reference guide for you to keep nearby when working through the Five Steps.

STEP 1: ASK

This step is to give you clarity on what you need to shift. Ask your energy a simple question to see if it's something you need to work on. For example, 'Am I holding any resistance or worry when I think about making more money?'

STEP 2: MOVE

Your energy body will respond and give you the 'yes' or 'no' answer to the question you asked. Forward is usually 'yes' and backward usually 'no'.

STEP 3: EXPERIENCE

This step is all about assessing what's happening in your energy when you think about that subject. You can perform this step in multiple ways. Today for this example just pay attention to how it makes you FEEL when you think about making more money.

Does it give you a tightness in your tummy or chest, heaviness in your legs? Just describe the physical sensations in your body. For example a tightness in your chest or a heaviness in your heart.

STEP 4: TRANSFORM

Now you Prepare and say your statement, '*I AM ready to release this tightness in my chest and dark black heaviness in my heart when I think about money. I release it from my energy in all forms, on all levels, and at all points in time.*' Repeat this at least three times or until you can no longer feel the resistant energy.

STEP 5: MANIFEST

Now you're ready to allow a new belief, thought or pattern. This time you get to choose what you experience in this case we want to have a better relationship with making more money. This is where you manifest your new future. It can be an emotion, belief thought, experience or anything you want to create.

Prepare and say your statement, for example '*I AM ready to Myself to feel happy and excited about making more money I allow this into my energy in all forms, on all levels, at all points in time.*' Repeat three times or more until you can feel that your energy is in alignment and you sway forward.

If you want to find out more about EAM and how to use it to shift your money blocks visit here:

www.energyalignmentmethod.com

to download a short programme to introduce you to the 5 steps of EAM and a list of 88 common limiting beliefs around money and new ones you can install to start transforming your relationship with money.

4

MY STORY PART 2

While working as a temp at the bank, we were not allowed to wear the bank's uniform. This was for staff only. This is a picture of me this first day I was given my uniform for the bank.

That is where my own career - my financial career- started. However, my financial story had only just started. One day travelling to work, I had a car accident. My old VW Polo was crushed in half from behind on an icy day by a driver apparently not looking at the road. My car was spun around, leaving me feeling like a crash-test dummy. The contents of the Polo were scattered all over the road -mainly CD's. Thankfully, I escaped with just bad whiplash, but in those days, you were sent on your way with little help. It took many years before my body was aligned and I could walk feeling straight and even. In the meantime, I took pain-killers to help with the terrible headaches.

During this time, I also met a boy, like you do, and we moved in together. Instead of saving to buy the furniture we needed, we took out an Argos store card. Sofas, tables, TV and bed, everything you would need to live comfortably. This was manageable but my spending continued with a car loan, after all, my old car had been written off. It didn't stop there. I justified my extravagance to myself as I was earning good money and could afford the monthly payments. The credit card debt started to build up as I brought lovely shoes and clothes. I was not buying cheap and cheerful, but top-of-the-range leather coats and handbags. Looking back, the reason I did this was to make myself feel better. I was in pain from my car accident and I enjoyed that initial buzz from having a lovely new pair of shoes. Having my hair done with a new outfit made me feel better, if only for a short while. But that was okay as I could go shopping again in a few days. I see women doing this at all ages, including spending on their children, not realising they are doing it. Happiness cannot come from a new pair of shoes but instead from making others happy. Can money buy happiness? They say "No", but you could buy a jet ski, or a horse in my case.

I partied every weekend, meals out and dancing to the early hours. We went on to buy our first flat for £118,000 in south-east London. My early twenties were a lot of fun. Even though I worked in a bank, this did not give me an education around money. I was taught to sell products, as are bank staff to this day. I knew what saving was and how it worked and I knew how loans and credit cards worked, I sold all these products for the bank.

But I woke up one day and realised it had gone too far and I had built up nearly £20,000 in debt without the new mortgage.

In this time, I had continued to work on my career and moved on to be an independent mortgage broker, earning good money for my age. I was promoted to a technical role in London and then was head-hunted into another mortgage brokerage firm, working my way up the ladder to become a team leader. The commission was getting better – and the more hours I put in, the more I earned. I was able to reduce the debt to a manageable level by using as much as possible of my commission to pay off the credit cards, just leaving my car loan outstanding. The boy I had moved in with had become my fiancé and we started to plan our wedding. This time, instead of paying for it using credit cards, I knew we had to save the money. We did just that. We paid for our wedding ourselves and our honeymoon to Disney, Las Vegas and New York. We had to make adjustments to our spending and make do with what we had. I had learnt to stop spending on credit cards and brought things when I had the money to do so. Simple, but a massive mindshift that was not easy.

While working in London and having this fantastic career, I did not realise at the time that I had become institutionalised by the industry. It was, and still is, a very male-dominated environment. I wore a shirt, I say that now and it sounds so weird, a T M Lewin shirt with cuff links. CUFF LINKS. I sometimes matched it with a pin-striped suit. Okay, this might be the 'thing to do' in London for men. The blacker the suit and the whiter the stripe, the better. But for a 25-year-old female? What was I thinking? The team were men aged 35-plus, and the management team were the same but older. It was such an environment that I did not see how masculine it was, and I became part of it. The way we were trained to speak to clients and recommend products was masculine. It was a fast and furious working place and, though the industry has calmed a little, the same training and practices are in place. I drew the line when one of the directors told me to go out to the sales floor - I was a sales manager at the time - take away an adviser's chair and "have a go at them" in front of everyone. The same director used to take advisers' chairs away from them if they did not make enough calls a day and come with a massive golf umbrella, slamming it on the top and shouting: "Do more, do more quickly."

I knew it was time to move on.

For a long time, I had tried to fit in, to be one of lads. But this was not as life was back when I was young,... being picked to play football. This was my adult life and it should have been on my terms. I continued to use the ethics my dad had taught me, which was work hard and do your best, not realising that actually, my best had reached a strong level. I was always pushing myself to do more or prove I was worth being listened to and that my opinion mattered.

Moving into my next role, still within financial services as a regional sales manager, the same ethos existed but there was a slightly nicer environment, and I was based from home. I enjoyed the diversity of the job and training new staff. My husband and I found out we were going to have our first baby. My manager at the time asked me to wait until I had to legally inform them and not before. I did not understand what he was hinting at or why he was acting in such a way, only later to find out that redundancies were on the cards for the company. However, I had read up on my rights and knew I have more rights if I told them. So, at 14 weeks, I officially informed them I was pregnant. But at 15 weeks, I was made redundant along with the other regional manager, therefore I had no legal position in terms of being pregnant as I was not being discriminated against.

I was shocked and disappointed. I didn't know what the future held. But I took it in my stride, hoping for a new opportunity elsewhere. As my bump grew and I was looking for opportunities, the reality of my situation sank in. Who wanted to employ a pregnant woman? I got in contact with past colleagues and discovered the industry was not doing so well in general, there was little contracting work or employed work.

After my daughter was born in 2008, the recession was officially announced and no one was taking on any work. Thousands of mortgage brokers and IFA's left the industry as business dried up. I started to apply for jobs outside the sector, looking for something different. Maybe something new that I had not come across before. I applied for what seemed like hundreds of jobs, in the end, signing on the dole. The humbling experience of the Job Centre, from the other side of the counter, is not something I would like to repeat ever again. I took a folder with me and a copy of all the jobs I had applied for plus the follow-up notes. The staff did not know what to do with me. Did you know you cannot take an umbrella into the main area in case you attack the staff with it? You have to leave it with security. I felt my career was over. My identity had been taken away. All those years of hard work for nothing. Many mums choose to stay at home and they thrive on it, enjoying every moment and wanting to do it with more children. But this was not the route I wanted to go down. I loved my time with my daughter but found the days long and missed my work purpose. I believed I could do both, but I had no idea how. I also wanted my own money and independence. I did not want my husband paying for me. I saw too many women puzzling what to do next when their children became teenagers. Many felt they had missed out.

My family encouraged me to "go back and work in a bank", back to my roots. A couple of banks locally were looking for staff and I managed to get a job interview at one. Expecting an online or computer-based technical interview and a face-to-face conversation, I was shocked to be presented at the first stage of interviews with an off-the-cuff mathematical test. My baby brain was still popping up whenever it was not needed and, of course, it did so at this interview. I was given a piece of paper and pencil to make notes and I was asked: "A client comes into the bank with 20 £20 notes, 15 £5 notes and 12 bags of £1 coins worth £20 each, he wants to deposit the money into his account and take out £276 using only £20 notes and some light change, how much would be left in his account if they had a balance starting at £75?" I had a minute to give an answer while the person was sitting watching what I wrote and worked out. Anyone would have struggled. But because of the place I was in at the time, I took it as a personal failure. After all, I had worked at a senior level in a bank and more senior roles elsewhere. A cashier in a bank was going back several steps and I could not do it. After four questions, I stopped the interview and walked home crying. I remember it well. It was raining and cried the whole way up Bexleyheath high street in Kent.

We all have those moments where we feel like it could not get any lower. That was one. My husband, ever supportive, told me not to worry and everything would be okay. But I could not see it. It was like I was under water and I could not hear what was being said, though I heard the tone being empathic and supportive. I was not able to take it on board.

After six months of signing on, I applied for a part-time, 14 hours, office administrator role for a charity. I got an interview, which amazed me as most people so far had not considered me even for an interview, mainly as I was over qualified. I got the job and it was perfect for me to rebuild my skills and confidence. I kept my head down and did my work and went home. It was not the dream role and it did not fulfil my soul but it gave me purpose and focus... and a belief that I was worth something. I appreciated that. After a year, I had found my feet and was more involved with the charity. I would have happily become their fund-raising person as I was confident in drumming up interest and it was for a charity – but there was not a role for me doing that. The administration role became repetitive, sending out the same letters for the same things, week in week out.

Then, my old boss asked if I wanted to join a team of insurance brokers he was putting together. It was one of those defining moments where it could all go very right or very wrong. I turned him down a few times, still not confident enough to get back into the saddle, but in the end, I went for it. I knew that I would not be content at the charity long term, and that I had tried most other industries, getting nowhere. It was time to take that leap - to push myself - if I wanted more. The first few months, I was like a duck out of water; everything felt familiar but I was not as clear or confident as before when it seemed like something I did with my eyes closed. Self-doubt kicked in often. The love of working with clients again however, was brilliant and easy. I went to people's homes and had a chat with them about their family, about what concerned them. I felt valued, like I was doing something worthwhile again. It is an amazing thing when you find something you believe in and you are appreciated for it. All the money in the world cannot pay that.

Unfortunately, the team was closed down but I was invited to join the main company unit, doing what I was already doing but adding mortgages to it, which obviously was my thing from a long time previously. Again, I thrived, but something was not right. I loved the job and I was paid well for it. What more could I ask for? But I could not sleep at night. I would lie awake feeling that something was not right. The firm I worked for, self-employed, would micro manage everyone, expecting 30-page client documents back into the office by 10am the next day, when you had seen the client only the night before. I would watch my little girl playing on the carpet while I had to get these reports done, feeling such guilt and anger as it just was not necessary to be managed in such a way. The situation went against everything I felt was right when it came to working WITH people - that collaboration and team work were key, not pushing to get the results you wanted. On top of this, I would be questioned on why certain products were "sold" to clients. Now firstly, I do not feel any product is sold to anyone; there is a need and if it is needed then the client has the option to take the recommendation. However, certain firms will have key indicators that are used from a sales perspective just to ensure they are getting the maximum revenue, without any real consideration for the client's needs. It reminded me of my time back in London and the industry as a whole.

I was left wondering again what my next move was going to be. I had tried other job applications in different industries and I knew the way I did things was appreciated by clients. Why should I leave the industry and start again because I could not find a position? Herein lies why so many women leave the financial services, especially adviser-type firms and roles. If they are not already established in their own right, they will not have the confidence to do this once they have children, often even without having children. I was not going to accept second best any longer. I was not going accept it was just how it was. Institutionalised or not, I wanted things done on my terms, with how I wanted to work with advisers and with my clients. From somewhere, I found the strength to believe that I could do it myself, that if anyone was going to make a difference and stand for something positive, it was going to be me. I had done it for other firms,...so why not for myself?

Yet if I thought I had already experienced a journey with a story to tell, as we all have, starting a business was, along with being a parent, the biggest challenge I had undertaken.

The roller coaster of emotions over these years was pretty crazy. My worst time was when I was a new mum with no job and being ill with a thyroid issue, having to have an operation and feeling really let down by everyone. It brought back a lot of emotions of not feeling good enough. I'd worked HARD to get to where I was and it was for nothing. I was nothing. It took years to get over that, by working HARD and having this feeling of constantly pushing to prove myself.

The way we are triggered and emotionally connected to ourselves will show up in our money and how we bring financial abundance to our lives.

5

FINANCIAL EMOTIONAL INTELLIGENCE

Most women make decisions based on Emotional Intelligence (EI). This is the capacity of individuals to recognise their own and other people's emotions, to discriminate between different feelings and label them appropriately. We use EI to guide thinking and behaviour, to manage and/or adjust emotions to adapt environments or achieve our goal(s). It's all about the 'feels'.

Understanding our money blocks, learning to put our money triggers aside and responding from our gut instinct is not something everyone is consciously aware they can do or even maybe that they are doing.

There are four key ways these blocks will be showing up today.

Number one: Miss aligned.

You are not feeling happy with your finances, meaning you have no emotional connection or, if I asked you to look at your bank account, you would feel annoyed at doing so, not necessarily because you have little in it.

This will be due to you not feeling aligned with your finances. You are spending money in areas of your life that do not make you happy and you see no benefit from them. You have to ensure you understand your values towards money and adjust your actions accordingly to them.

- **Be strong to your values – know what you want.**

Number two: Past expectations.

You are operating (spending and earning) in a way that is comfortable to other people's expectations of you or your own based on your self confidence.

Often, we do not like to step out and be different from our friends and family. We don't want to be seen as different, weird maybe? We can spend money in ways that are just what everyone else around us is doing.

It is not what we want for ourselves. Equally, we can earn money based on what those around us earn, not thinking we could have to do more.

- **Let go of past expectations – set your own rules.**

Number three: Avoidance.

Avoidance, or dealing with your finances in a passive nature, can cause more stress. This could be a failure to ring the bank to extend your overdraft or to call the pension company to work out your figures. Just hoping it will all be okay, or that the universe will do it for us - often there are signs every day which are there but we just are not seeing or feeling them. Especially in relationships. This can cause much frustration and more stress as the other person wants to resolve issues or come to a conclusion.

- **Stop avoiding actions – be honest and take a small action today.**

Number Four: Enoughness.

I am too old, I am too poor, I am too short, I am not worthy. Enoughness is where you feel you're not good enough for something. No matter your place in life, we all have an upper ceiling and the essence is working out when you have reached it? Is that earning £10,000 a year, a month, or a week? What do you feel is possible for you?

- **Money and Wealth is for you too.**

So, which of those four are you?

Miss aligned – Past expectations – Avoidance – Enoughness

Financial Emotional Intelligence

Many female clients want to understand the full spectrum of information, not just the top three or four facts of how much are the costs, how much was last year's returns and what is the volatility rate?

This can be misunderstood for questioning an expert but it is, in fact, how we process the information to then make an informed decision based on how we feel about it. Women tend to avoid these decisions if they do not understand all the facts, thus causing procrastination and being overwhelmed.

Women ask many questions of themselves when making financial decisions, such as:

1. How will this affect the family?
2. How will this affect me, long term?
3. How will this affect our monthly position?
4. How will this affect my goals?
5. Is this ethical and right?
6. Am I able to do this?

By doing so, they are taking into account not just their own position, but they are wanting to ensure all elements are being considered. These will include: affordability; what cover is in place; what work may do for me; what investments already exist and whether the return these provide is enough; how this will impact the children; does this fit in with our other goals; will it stop us from achieving elsewhere?

Therefore, financial intelligence does not come naturally to anyone; you have to learn it and develop the skills to understand it.

Once you have looked at your money blocks, you can then start to increase your Financial Emotional Intelligence by learning and understanding a number of areas of finances to allow you to make informed decisions.

And here is your second of 10 ways to accelerate your wealth –

Number 2:

What does being financially emotionally intelligent mean to you?

Think of a woman and what she would do every day, week or month to be FEI? What would she wear, eat or listen to? Who would she have around her, spend time with and invite out for dinner? How would she consider increasing her FEI?

Write out those ideas and consider what you would like to do yourself?

What could you do today to increase you FEI?

Additionally, now considering the four previous money blocks, what do you need to let go of and start taking responsibility for?

- Your self-worth?
- Taking action?
- Knowing your values?
- Setting your own rules?

What actions could you do today to set a new or stronger path?

6

FINANCIAL ABUNDANCE MATRIX

There is a natural way that when you grow into wealth – that is, you are not born into it, or given large sums of money – that you evolve through the stages of that wealth. We do not just wake up one morning and embrace it all perfectly. We gradually learn, make mistakes and take the next steps to grow in our abundance.

I have created the Financial Abundance Matrix. This details the stages of wealth, in conjunction with how we are feeling about our finances, not just the amount of money in our bank account. However, what feels like success to one person, is not the same for the next. The stages are not hierarchical – meaning a top and a bottom. I believe that everyone is equal and we can all work together. One stage is not better than the other - we can go on to the final stage of wealth and can come back round again, beginning again as we grow outside our comfort areas. It is a circle... and it is part of life.

1st stage: Evasion

Now, this is where you are in a dependent state. You are avoiding any form of money decisions. You are maybe leaving envelopes in drawers; you are not checking bank statements. You have only a very small form of income, and that is okay, but it is maybe coming from one source, which you are reliant on. It might be even one thing from a partner or a parent or you have got only one job that you can do. So, it is quite a place of limitation and you are in a mindset where you are avoiding any sort of conversations, any sort of need or requirement to be able to grow or build from there and quite often you are in a place where there is a lot of blame going on, where you are blaming other people. You are putting the ownership on to other people and there is no real responsibility for where you are at. It can be a case that you can have debts and it may be that your outgoings are exceeding the income coming in. This is not a fun place to be. But we have all been there, we have all had difficult times. The question is: What can you do to move things onto the next stage?

2nd stage: Conscious

You start to become more conscious about your spending, about what debts you have, and conscious about how you think and feel about your money. This is where you might have started to look at the debts and put a better plan in place to be able to clear them. Do you have an ultimate goal? You might not have cleared your debts but you are in a place where you feel that you are growing towards clearing them off. These debts can sometimes span a long period but you, certainly at conscious level, are able to look at what you have in place, how you are servicing them, and how you are going to clear them.

If there are no debts, you are aware that you need to consider saving or start to put small procedures in place to make sure you move in the right direction. Perhaps by earning more and developing your business or career towards higher earnings.

You may have built up clutter at home, keeping things around you to make you feel 'full'. You might believe that your never win anything or allow money to come to you easily in different ways, like someone buying you dinner.

3rd stage: Sense of surroundings

You may have increased your revenue or salary. You are considering what income you would like and how you want your career or business to move into higher earnings. You are maybe thinking about what the next career step is. You have started to look at your spending habits and begun to think about your expenditure. You are reading the bank statements. You are looking at the bills that comes in. You are starting to have a much higher awareness and conscious mindset around money. So, the next level is a real sense of stability, not quite full financial security but a position from where you have a genuine plan towards addressing your debts, perhaps possibly even paid them off. You are feeling more confident about your decision making. You may have a mortgage, for example, but you will have money to fall back on. There is a buffer in place if something was to happen. You have a sense of stability when it comes to understanding what monies are going out. You have cash flow plots in position.

You start to clear the clutter around you, you start to shred paperwork and clear out rooms filled with items you no longer need . You begin to feel anything is possible... and you could win a free holiday away tomorrow, why not?

4th stage: Stability

You have more coming in than you have going out and you have maybe started to think about wills and life insurance and talking to your workplace about your pension. If you are in business, you have looked back at some old pensions and start to remember when your accountant mentioned something about them. You should do something about it. You are starting to acquire a sense of stability and you start to feel proud of yourself, that you can breathe above water and you are not bobbing up and down out of the murky depths anymore. You have a buoyancy aid on and you are floating comfortably and it does not feel quite so much of a struggle.

What is important at this point is that you continue to thrive and you do not get to a stage where you could potentially slip back under the water. You have to stay in that space by keeping your focus

If you want to be extremely healthy – perhaps by not eating burgers for breakfast or refraining from drinking alcohol or smoking – you can achieve that. But then, if all of a sudden you think, 'I won't bother with that anymore, I do not need to do that now', you will return to all those bad habits. It is the same with money. If you have bad habits, you can slip into your old ways by over spending and not making the best-informed decisions.

5th stage: Reassurance

You might not be quite at the stage of planning for kids to go to university but you are at a point of making sure you have a buffer, some money in the bank. If anything was to happen, you be able to look after yourself. The next stage from here however, is security... or reassurance, as I call it. You are feeling quite reassured in yourself, when it comes to your finances. If something was to happen, you could pack in your job and still have enough money saved to cover three or six months of outgoings, taking the worry out of what might happen. The figure of reassurance can vary for people, depending on their level of risk and how much risk they like to take, and how much security will make them feel comfortable.

Once you have had the reassurance for a while, you can start to feel you are not achieving maximum benefit from those reserves. They are rather going to waste, not least as interest rates are so low. You can then move on to thinking about how you could grow that money.

You feel like you have not just a buoyancy aid, but you are in a boat now, safe and dry. If you have a hole in that boat, you have a life-raft with you just in case. You would likely have cleared your debts but maybe still have a mortgage in place. There can be times where there is good debt. Using money that is growing against something that is being charged very little interest rate is not always a bad thing. It is just making sure you are not living beyond your means in regards to servicing debts and repaying them. Here, you would start to focus more on your future. You would be thinking, perhaps, about paying for the kids to go to university, upgrading to a larger property, starting a first or second business, or buying that second home. You will be thinking longer term about retirement and truly developing a life-plan strategy.

Lifestyle financial planning. What I see people do in this phase is to start spending unnecessarily. Because they have the money, they just spend it, not really being conscious of the expenditure. They have bad habits left over from past stages of wealth.

Though their bank balance has moved on, their mindset has not and they are reverting to those old ways. This stifles the growth because you then get to the end of the year, or another focal point, and you wonder where has all the money gone?

We should be considering the building of other forms of revenue and income that would allow us to leverage our position further.

6th Stage: Independence

We can spend unnecessarily on things that are not really going to support our growth, but you move on to the next phase, independence. This is where you are not relying on one job or one income or one business, you have enough to live off, and it does not just support your standard of living, you could stop work and you would still have enough money to live on.

It is a big jump from reassurance to independent. You are not relying on parents, you are not relying on partners, you are not relying on one thing particular thing. You have all your plans in place and you are accumulating assets that will in turn bring wealth and income for you. The question is, how long could you do that job or business for? You do not want to be doing it in your 70s and your 80s.

So, it is about creating assets before you get to that certain age.

Financial freedom, which is a terminology I do not particularly like, is about creating assets outside of that dependence. So you are not having to do podcasts or YouTube's in your 70s, or working in a job you hate up to, or past, your state retirement age. Instead, you are at a point of financial independence where you are more than comfortable and you are able to enjoy a life in which you make your own choices.

7th and final stage: Abundance

You have reached a point where you could, at the drop of a hat, hire a yacht somewhere, which is abundance. You could go on holiday for a month and not think twice about it. In fact, your whole life feels like a holiday.

But abundance for me, sits in the middle. It overlaps all the areas because you cannot move on to the next step without having that positive abundance mindset and thinking positively about things; letting go of the past and being able to move on to that next stage. To be in true abundance in the financial wealth sense means that you have income from all sources, not only to fulfil your lifestyle but to grant you freedom and choice to do whatever you want, when you want.

What stage do you think you are at right now?

What things could you start to do to move yourself on to the next stage?

It is imperative that, whatever the answers are, you take action. If you do not take consistent action on a regular basis, you are only going to recreate those habits over and over again, and repeat the same cycles, not only with yourself but those around you.

7

MY MONEY STORY PART 3

The summer of 2011 is when I officially started my own business. Prior to being made redundant, I was firmly making my way into the reassurance phase. However, launching a business and having a baby set me back for some time.

I began with just a few friends and family at a working men's club, giving a short presentation on financial planning. The evening was a success so, two months later, I did another event. However, I did not know any more people than previously so I had the same crowd come along, barring a few additions. It cost me money with food and drinks but it was enjoyable. In between these events, I paid to spend a couple of days at Orpington Shopping Centre in Kent, being one of those annoying people who approach you when you are not interested, even if you were being offered free gold. I learnt a lot but that venue did not work and I found the process and effort unrewarding. If you do not love doing it or you are not buzzing from it, what is the point? The idea was right but I just did not achieve the correct results.

The following month, I found myself networking. I started picking up ideas about email marketing and created a Mail-Chimp account to contact people regularly. In the January, I found myself at a psychic fair where, amazingly, I managed to pick up some leads. But I realised I was not reaching my target market. I was also going to ladies pamper events, and on my stand I had a lovely pamper basket to win in a prize draw. I had lots of entries and I was picking up leads but I still felt the level of work and effort was not being rewarded. It was not progressing in the direction I had envisaged. The same went for wedding shows. I thought I would be hitting a target market there but my timing was off. The couples were interested only in the fancy parts of getting married, few took the financial planning element seriously.

I went back to where I started and I ran another event called 'Empowering women networking'. My friends had grown bored of my business by now and I found the new people supporting me were other businesswomen. Ten or so people came but again, it cost me money to put on the event with little return. I could not spend another month promoting and financing the venture when it was not producing anything new, apart from the networking element.

I was back into the 'sense' stage of wealth, very aware that I was not earning and everything was outlay. Building up my marketing confidence and learning to gain my own clients was draining resources and I was starting to slip back into those enoughness habits, where my money mindset was becoming smaller and smaller.

We were now heading for Easter 2012. I was using social media more and the list was getting longer and more daunting. LinkedIn, a Facebook page and profile groups, such as Pinterest, Twitter and WordPress as well as blogs, a website and SEO. I continued to try these different platforms to see which worked and which were too time-consuming. I was also drilling down into my market more and I stopped attending wedding fairs and such like. Instead, I was focusing on the new-baby market, attending larger events in Kent and local smaller events in the Medway area. At some of these, I was getting 250-plus email addresses. However, after a year of working this marketing and attending events, gathering more than 700 email addresses, I realised timing is key. If you are in your target marketing place when someone's buying time is off, the exercise is pointless. I still communicate with all those people via my MailChimp newsletter.

I continued to focus on the baby market and I was getting busier and busier, building a strong online following. I opened up a small office space in the September as my daughter had started school. I developed the networking and the idea of the events by creating a non-profit 'networking women in business' group. In the January 2013, I employed an apprentice and everything was progressing well. I did not appreciate this at the time, but you never do. You are just hoping and dreaming about pushing the business forward.

This I did, but I always coming from a place of 'lack and not enough'. The business was not making enough and I was still pushing to prove so much to myself, that I was good enough.

In the June, the new baby market went quiet. I had tons of ideas but I was tired. The thought of starting another project was not appealing. Then, the kids were having the end of school fairs and things became even quieter. What should I do? Act, that's what. I started listing myself in directories where I did not want to be before. I really had to drive myself to launch a new project. And being me, I did not start one, I started four. One of these was a money make-over system. I presented at a ladies' networking event and enjoyed the opportunity to help people with any questions or issues they may have.

In January 2014, I set myself the task to grow the business further, wanting to go from solo adviser to a team of advisers. I launched my recruitment event for April in London. It was a big step and outside my comfort zone, putting myself out there as a director of the company. I set about organising contracts, manuals and processes. It took over my summer but was proud of the end result. I had a 200-page manual, full of the knowledge I had acquired over my then 14 years' experience - now 21 years.

The team started and I continued to manage the business, overseeing the team while working with clients. It was stressful but the core objective was to create more jobs for women within financial services, providing more women with financial advice. It meant everything to me to make it work.

The learning curve over the following few years was steep. Working with driven women without any of the right boundaries in place for myself or the business meant I was being pushed and pulled in many directions. It all came back to my self-worth. I was willing to forgo my own needs for the success of others and making them happy. I would avoid any confrontation as I did not want to risk losing anyone. That would be viewed by me as a failure, before saying enough was enough.

I CONTINUED to fill my enoughness bucket with applying for multiple awards…

1. Independent Financial Adviser of the year 2019 – Women in Finance awards.
2. Role Model of the Year - Women in Financial Advice awards 2019.
3. Kent Women in Business 2016 – Women in Finance. Shortlisted.
4. Kent Women in Business 2016 – Customer Service Award. Shortlisted.
5. Professional Adviser 2016 – Personality of the Year. Shortlisted (out of 35,000 advisers plus).
6. Corporate Live Wire 2016 Innovation & Excellence Awards. Won Excellence in Financial Advisory Services for Women Award.
7. Kent Women in Business 2015 - Won Customer Service Award.
8. Kent Women in Business 2016 – Leadership and Management. Shortlisted.
9. Corporate Live Wire 2015 Innovation & Excellence awards – Shortlisted.
10. Kent Independent Traders Awards 2014 - Finalist 'Professional Business.
11. Kent Women in Business – Small Business Owner of the year 2014 - Runner Up.
12. Kent Independent Traders Awards 2013 - Finalist Business Growth.
13. Kent Independent Traders Awards 2013 - Runner up Customer Services.
14. Women in Finance/banking – 2012 Jo Cameron's Achievers Academy for Women.

After a Ted Talk, 'What if women ruled the world', and having another baby, I started to see the patterns and how I was not putting myself first while believing I was able and capable of anything I set my mind to.

The business scaled back from ten advisers at one point, to just me and one other. It turned out that 'less was more'. Organic growth, taking on advisers to support our clients when the business needed that, was the way forward.

Prior to my maternity leave in December 2015, the business was doing so well. I had months of money backed up and was paying myself more. I knew I had a model that worked and I was simply refining it.

I was expecting to come back to a full calendar of client work and a pipeline of paying clients. I felt I had done everything possible to ensure this was the case. What I did not take into account was people wanting to give me space as I had had a baby and I discovered leads had not been followed up. The result was I came back to zero clients and zero pipeline, with only a few months cashflow to cover.

All my previous money mindset issues – there is not enough and I am not worth more – came flooding back. I had to apply every skill I knew to get me through the following six months. I had learnt all the right principles but I had to apply them, and fast. I became extremely self-aware of my own money setbacks, catching myself when I found those little monsters in my head, telling me off.

I began to create more of the right clients, became super-focused in my marketing and I dropped all things that were not benefiting myself or the business. It sounds simple when you know how. I had spent long enough messing around.

I was building several revenue streams to the business and, for the first time, paying myself a proper full-time salary equivalent.

I have told how, as a young girl, I dreamed of being a vet but I realised that was not going to happen. That did not lessen my love of animals. I wanted to learn to be around horses and learn to ride them. This was possible only when my mum would buy me riding lessons for my birthday once a year.

I took up riding again when full-time employed before I had the children as I could afford several lessons a week. I loved it. For more than 11 years, I loaned several horses from private owners on and off, always wanting my own one day. It was never the right time. For me to feel I was ready and could afford it, I would need to be closer to financial independence. In October 2018, I bought my first horse, Goose, a three-year-old Connemara silver dun. A life-long dream had been achieved and I developed a real spending habit for rugs. I mean, how many does a horse really need?

Although I am not fully financially independent, as I have described in my stages previously, I could care for myself and my children should myself and my partner separate. We should never judge the financial choices of others but instead look to ourselves for what means the most to us.

And here is your third of 10 ways to accelerate your wealth –

Number 3:

What stage of the financial abundance matrix are you in?

What changes to you need to make? Declutter, shred and create space for?

What decisions are you avoiding or putting off? Do you need to pick up the phone and take action today?

What is next on the list to achieve the next stage of wealth?

What will make you happy? What will bring you joy? Increase the energy vibration and bring some exciting new things into your world?

8

MONEY MAKEOVER PROGRAMME™

This programme has been put together after many years' experience working with clients. The process is the one I have always taken clients back to and asked them to look over again, as their feelings and thoughts do not change around it but the habits they seem to create do. Consistency in your approach is vital.

Our Money Makeover Programme™ goes through five stages to help you change the way you feel about money in order to assist you in using it to your advantage. The five sections are:

Analyse,

Assess,

Compare,

Budget,

Plan.

We will look at how to give yourself a financial detox and start fresh with a new plan and a new commitment to improving your financial wellbeing.

Section 1: Analyse - What does money mean to you?

These exercises are best undertaken when you are in a quiet place with a note-book, something to refer back to.

To analyse your beliefs about money, take a moment to read these sayings: -

"Money means nothing to me"
"Money means everything to me"
"Money is anything"

What does money mean to you?

Do you feel that it means very little and how much you have in your bank account is no motivation? How long do you spend looking after your money – do you ignore it and put statements in the drawer?

Or do you love money? Do you look at your bank statements or online apps every day? Do you watch every penny?

Or is it that money gives you the ability to purchase certain items that make you happy? New shoes or another dress? Maybe you like to spend money on others, such as family?

Or is money everything to you? Do you love it so much that you collect it under the mattress or in a bank account?

Or is money a facilitator to enable you to live a life of your choosing?

Money is not always about the physical amount in your bank balance but it can be the time we take out of the working day to help others. Time is money after all...

Or it might mean giving to a charity.

To me, money is grease, like putting oil on the wheels of a bike. It allows us to live a certain life and provide us with the tools to be comfortable, now and in the future.

What do you believe about money?

Going back to my story, I described my childhood as having two financial elements, one of my dad's and one of my mum's, both having different lifestyles. Holidays were a good example. My dad would take us camping and we would drive to France, whereas my mum would fly abroad and stay in nice hotels.

Think about your childhood memories, where did your family take you on holiday? What did your parents do over the school summer holidays? What did your parents do with their money? Did they have a love or hate relationship with it?

We were not taught at school how to manage our finances, we learned from our family. We learned from their approach to money. Did your parents give you money without any questions? Did your mum or dad put money in the bank or under the mattress? Did they have a large property or more than one property? Your subconscious acts due to these past memories. We act in our early working years based on the past, either in a positive or negative manner. We continued our self-education after making mistakes and trying to rectify those mistakes.

I used to feel that I did not deserve nice things, that they were for other people. Even now, as I spend money on renovating my house, buying high quality to ensure it lasts often means greater expense. When we stop to think, we realise that such thoughts and decisions are our own limiting beliefs. We have inherited them. These thoughts have created habits that we might not even be aware about.

To help you become more alert to these potential habits, start making a note of some of the things we have mentioned. Do you look at the bank statements? Do you check your balance before you buy something? When was the last time you treated yourself? Some people put up post-it notes around the house to help remind them.

Once you start to know the answers to these questions, you will become more aware of how you feel about money. Are you a money hater or a money lover?

Clients who have had the best results have had certain things in common. First, if you do not have a clear goal and a strong determination to bring about change, the likelihood of any alterations staying long term is very low. I sat with a couple where she was sure her partner would not make any changes to enable them to carry out their house extension, as it meant they would incur new monthly mortgage payments. For a year, they had been in a stand-off avoiding the subject. He was not wanting to be forced into giving up the little treats he allowed himself and the family. Their joint credit card was always needing clearing down, which she was doing away with the savings she made each month. You see the cycle.

By following some of the exercises later in this programme, we were able to find middle ground and a compromise. What was frustrating was that they both had the same goal and the motivation... but the 'how' was the major obstacle. Exactly what adjustments were they going to make to their existing habits? With this couple, one small sticking-point was how much he spent on lunches. Hundreds of pounds were being laid out in McDonald's and coffee shops every month. And yet they were not able to go on a skiing holiday as they could not afford it. We changed the habit. His wife was more than happy to add his lunch needs to those of the children and, though it would cost her more money, it would save the family overall... as then he could contribute more. The habit of going out to purchase lunch was taken away.

This pattern of 'lacking' is one I see all the time with clients. They feel they cannot afford a holiday, a new car or to move house, etc. However, they spend money on things they cannot even remember.

Usually, men who like gadgets will justify unnecessary products claiming they NEED them when, in fact, they do not NEED them but they WANT them. There is a huge difference.

In reality, many clients do not know where anything from £200 to £1,200 a month is spent. This is due to failing to have an identification with their money. They simply spend it. Having a goal, something you can identify with emotionally or even physically, is the most practical way to change this situation.

When do we stop and analyse where we are with our finances? After a year, looking back and wanting more? Inheriting money from a family member and spending it within a few months but being unable to account for what you spent the money on? When we lose our job and have to take a lower paid one? When we separate from our partner and our house money is halved? There can be a number of events that happen in our life time.

If we analysed our finances more often, would they be in a better position? I think so.

Exercise 1

This first exercise is designed to help you analyse your beliefs about money.

So many people dream of winning the Lottery, though we have all read a number of stories about millions being wasted and not looked after properly. But just imagine you won £150,000. Imagine what you could do with it. Buy that new car, take the family on holiday and put in the new kitchen.

Write a list of six things, in order of priority, that you would spend the winnings on? Take your time, really think about it. What would you do with all that money? Once you have written these, think about the following questions:

- What does the list tell you about yourself?
- Have you spent the money on yourself or on someone else?
- Have you invested it or have you spent it on nice things?

What do the results tell you about your beliefs?

Let me help you with this. We usually have four reasons for making financial decisions: spending, purchasing, investing and hoarding.

Spending is food and shopping; purchasing is insurance or cars or houses; investing is a pension or stock/shares or an ISA; and hoarding is under the mattress or in a jam-jar.

Spending is low down the rationality scale, meaning it does not last that long and is impulsive. Whereas investing is longer term and well thought out.

So, now we go back to your six things you would purchase:

* How rational where these purchases? Have you spent all your money on short-term impulse buys low down the rationality? Or have you invested it all?

I do not believe anyone who has done this exercise has answered that they invested it all.

Life is about balance, the time we spend with our loved ones versus the time we spend at work. If we spend too much time on one thing, the other suffers. It is the same with money, we need to balance our spending and saving to have a balanced financial life.

How have you balanced your wish list?

The more money we have, the more decisions we have to make. I have already alluded to millionaires who go bankrupt due to a failure to monitor their spending. What they really should have done was increase their financial IQ to achieve a more balanced approach to their money.

Section 2: Assess - What are your personal values?

We have looked at what you believe about money, talking about your childhood and asking on what you would spend your money on if you won the Lottery. Now we are going to look at your personal values.

Exercise 1

I would like you to draw two columns on a piece of paper. On one side write 'What do I have?' and on the other side 'What don't I have?' These questions relate to financial matters, of course.

What DO I have?	What DON'T I have?

We spend a lot of our time thinking about what we don't have, thinking of what we want to buy next and what our neighbour has. Basically, comparing ourselves to others. We spend less time appreciating what we do have.

You might list that you do have a roof over your head, a nice car, a happy family and animals. You might put you don't have a new kitchen or a holiday planned.

Exercise 2

This exercise is about enlightening: What are your personal values? When it comes to these, they will fit into one of these ten categories:

- Creativity/personal expression. This could be in any form, such as acting, painting, speaking or dancing.
- Professional development. This could be paying for a course, reading, paying for a mentor or going back to school.
- Growth of self. This could be travelling or starting a new job or working for a charity.
- Family. This could be spending more time with loved ones or providing for them.
- Relationships. This could be going out with friends, treating a boyfriend or husband, or this could be spending time with your partner.

- Health. This could be a gym membership or using a personal trainer or having regular check-ups or paying for supplements
- Independence. This could mean a passive income (not an hourly rate income) or having your own space to live without having to rely on someone else.
- Personal legacy. This could be your long-term legacy for the world or your family.
- Sense of control. This means you having full awareness and the ability to make decisions without worries.
- Security. This could mean more than having a roof over your head but feeling safe at home and your future being safe and secure.

These words should have your own meaning and resonate with you on your own level.

Independence and security can often mean the same to some people; think back to the stages of wealth and how you want to feel about your finances.

Now you need to decide what your top five personal values are. Don't think long about this, the five should be the first things that come into your mind. Then order them, one to five, with the first being the most important to you.

Section 3: Compare – What you want compared to your personal values?

We are now going to compare your values. Let's look back at the exercise. The list of 'What do I have?' itemises your main assets.

Exercise 1

Compare this list main asset list to your top five personal values.

For example:

Roof over my head - security

New Car - creative expression

Does this asset list cover all top five values?

What is missing for you?

What are you currently spending on, each month or year, that is not aligned to these values?

How can we be happy in life if we are spending all of our time creating things for ourselves that do not match our personal values? We can't. Time and money need to be spent on what is important to us, really important.

I find a lot of clients have a nice car and a nice home, however when looking at their personal values, more often than not they do not compare to what they do have in life. I see this with single women in their 30s. Lots of lovely things to talk about having, such as cars and shoes, but when looking at their values, independence is important to them. Their spending or focus is not anywhere near becoming independent -usually, they do not know where to start.

Often money is the pillar of people's happiness, not because money is important but because they are spending money in areas that are not actually important to them. For example, if they think about learning a new skill and taking piano lessons, they think "I can't afford it" when in fact, they can afford it. They simply have the wrong focus and they do not realise it.

Habits we create with our personal spending filter into our business spending. For those who are business owners, we often use our business bank account as a bank account for personal expression and personal development. I believe in investing in yourself, I've done that to get to where I am today, but we need to know when to stop.

For new habits to be created, we must value money, have the right environment and a clear goal.

Section 4: Budget – Budget with a twist.

Knowing where your spending is focused right now is a key element in mastering your money. How will you know what habits to change? How will you know what cut backs to make, if any? How will you see where you are not concentrating enough attention?

What are you investing/spending money in currently and where is that against your personal values?

Exercise 1

If done correctly, this can add so much value to your finances, not just currently but in the long term. It is like a business audit, no one wants to do it but once it is done you are pleased to know what needs to change and how well, in reality, you are doing. Some clients are doing a lot better than they believe they are.

The best way to start is to print off three months bank statements for yourself and your partner's income, if you wish to do this as a household. It can be a positive exercise for you to do together, though I have been to clients' houses when, once the partner is out the room, I've been told about loans and credit cards that the other did not know about. This is not a good place to be with your money.

This can also be done the same way for business finances.

Once you have printed off the bank statements, run through the transactions putting each one into a section.

1. Fixed expenditures. These are outgoings that are normally monthly commitments, for example mortgage or council tax
2. Set expenditures. You know where the money is spent but you do not know the amounts, for example petrol or eating out. By making a note of these for past three months, you can average them out to a monthly total.
3. Essential and non-essential items. These are the items that take a little more work, they are often small things and lots of them. Again, they need to be added up, they might even end up with a place on your budget planner all on their own, such as Costa Coffee, if you go there enough. Again, you can average this out into a monthly spend.

Some people like to write it all down. If this is you, use a bound note book as you will want to look back on this. Using your PC is easier as you can save the document – and by using the Excel program, this will add up the totals for you.

This will provide totals, deduct the income and work out the surplus. There is also a free budgeting video to help you know where things are and where to place items.

Once you know what is going out each month and how much is coming in, you will know how much surplus cash you have. If you don't have any surplus, but your calculations are showing you should have, you need to go back to your bank statements and make sure you have not missed items.

Budgets need to be made and planned into our daily lives. This gives us a framework to work around to make sure that we do not spend outside our means and that we know exactly what is in the bank at any one time.

Now put your spending items into one of the 10 personal value areas:

- Creativity/personal expression,
- Professional development,
- Growth of self,
- Family,
- Relationships,
- Health,
- Independence,
- Personal legacy,
- Sense of control,
- Security.

You then tally up the totals to establish your top five.

Compare this to your original list.

How many match up? What isn't in place? What is missing?

Section 5: Plan – Only action makes change happen.

Only action will make changes and it takes six to eight weeks to create new habits.

And here is your fourth of 10 ways to accelerate your wealth –

Number 4:

Take a look at your outgoings. What needs to change within your current spending procedure? Where do you need to focus your financial efforts? How can you make those changes?

Something I give a lot of my clients to do is a Financial Detox. This is a great way to get a handle on the changes that need to be implemented. I suggest a three-month programme.

MONTH 1

Using the budget planner, you have completed and using different ways to make cut-backs (listed further on), plus seeing what you could instigate reductions on, such as making lunches and only eating out once a month, reset your budget to a DETOX budget. Try to increase the spare capital to 20% of your salary. So, if you earn £1,000 a month this would be £200.

The amount will then become your savings. If you have not saved before, you will need a section on your planner for this. If you have saved previously, try to increase the gap by 20%.

To ensure there is no over-spending, a lot of clients withdraw the amount they are budgeting to save and place the cash in

separate jars. Spending within the 'allowance' for any particular item ensures the overall budgeting is adhered to. Once the
jar is empty, you do not put more in.

It is important to tell family and friends what you are planning.
This is not about you being lacking in any way, but about you
wanting to improve and take positive steps towards your financial freedom. Knowing what parties are coming up and what
meals out you have planned is key. And if you have forgotten to
put one in the budget, be prepared to tell the hosts you cannot
make it. Have the conviction to follow through with your plan.
You will only be cheating yourself if you do otherwise.

Another great way to understand your finances better is to have
a note pad at hand – in your bag, on the kitchen side or at your
desk at work – to compile a list of items that you DIDN'T buy.
These are items you would have normally purchased. Maybe
you even missed them off your bank statements when
reviewing your out-goings. This is your spending journal. Make
a note next to each item if it was something you WANTED or
something you NEEDED. At the end of the month, add up the
total to see how much you would have spent. If you still NEED
those items listed, the decision is yours on whether to go ahead
with the purchase.

MONTH 2:

Here, you can treat yourself. Give yourself an allowance to
have an extra meal out or a day trip for the family. This is, of
course, if you have been strict enough in your detox month.
You may have found some additional ways to make adjustments to provide you additional savings.

Set your revised budget, use the jars to manage the cash flow if
needed and put aside those savings.

MONTH 3:

By now, you will be a professional budgeteer. This is not about being frugal but about knowing where all your money goes. This is the foundation needed to be able to start to plan the next phase. The quicker you can get here the better.

You now have a money management plan. You have the foundation to build and take things to the next level. You can start treating yourself to that new bag or saving for that holiday.

Your confidence will increase and your will feel so much more empowered with your finances.

MORE MONEY SAVING IDEAS:

Saving on energy bills.

You can change spending habits if you look at your house and go round room by room. There are little things you can do to save money on your energy bills:

- Turn down your thermostat.
- Close the curtains as the sun goes down to stop the heat escaping.
- Turn off the lights when you leave a room.
- Turn off the TV when no one is watching it.
- Don't leave items on charge unnecessarily.
- Fill up your washing machine or dishwasher, they use less water and electricity on one full load than two half loads.
- Make sure none of your taps drip.

You can get a free energy check from the Energy Saving Trust website, which gives you a free report on how you can save money on your bills.

Saving on shopping.

- If your journey to work sends you through a shopping centre, change your route to work if you can.
- Tell your friends that you are going out for dinner only once a month instead of once a fortnight.
- Meet your friends in their homes or your home instead of in the coffee shop.
- When you are food shopping, try some of the shop's own brand items, they can be just as good yet half the price.
- If you want to buy new clothes, think about what is already in your wardrobe. Is there anything that you could sell to make some money to buy the new item? Does it go with what you have in your wardrobe? Will you wear it once and then leave it because you have not got anything to wear it with.
- Cut up your credit cards. Maybe keep one for emergencies, but put it away in a box so it's harder to get to it.
- Apply for a 0% interest rate card and transfer your balance from your current card.

Saving on investments and insurances.

Many people overpay on life insurance policies for years without realising. It is well worth getting a fresh eye to look at your policies and see whether they are relevant for you now and whether they could cost you less.

Examine cash ISAs to see if they are still as effective as they were when you took them out. ISA interest rates change all the time and you could be losing out.

General savvy saving tips.

Set aside as much of your salary as you can for saving and investing, even if it's only a few pounds, as it will add up over time. A general good rule is to have three months' essential outgoings in a savings account for emergencies.

Build up an emergency fund from one of your guilty pleasures. Look at what you spend out for something that is really unnecessary, such as a takeaway coffee every morning or that takeaway meal during the week because you cannot be bothered to cook. It may sound small but the amount will build up over time and you will be surprised at how much you can save.

If you have some surplus money to put away each month, use it first to start paying off the highest interest debt you have. Getting rid of a debt quickly is better for you in the long term, and then you can invest more as you do not have that monthly payment to contend with.

So, where do you begin?

The best way to start is to set a goal for yourself, something that you really would like for you and your family, such as a holiday abroad or a new car, something that really gives you a push to get moving.

Write it down, preferably where you all can see it every day – such as stuck to the fridge. This is a good way of reminding yourself why you are changing your habits.

Work out how much you are going to save. Even if it's a small amount, everything helps.

Find a money box or tin to put change into and leave it in an accessible place where you can easily put the coins but not be able to take them out so easily. Or set up a standing order straight from your bank account into a simple savings account, so you won't miss the money.

The state-owned National Savings and Investments bank (NS&I) states that people who set a savings goal save faster, and up to £550 a year more, than those who do not. So, get saving and change the habits of a lifetime.

Top tips for getting your finances under control and work your way out of debt.

Here are a few ways of getting our finances back into the black.

Look at your finances.

Take your head out of the sand and have a good look at your finances. Assemble all your paperwork. Find out exactly how much you owe and to whom. As a rule, if your debt repayments take up more than 20% of your total income, you really need to take steps to cut back.

Make a budget.

Once you know how much you owe, you can then set a monthly budget schedule for repaying those debts. Don't try to do it all at once because that could put you into a deeper mess. Work out a realistic monthly payment that you can afford. Talk to your creditors to see if you can agree a schedule of payments. Many welcome this step as they realise that you are serious about repaying the money.

Think before you spend.

Do not borrow any more money or take on any more loans or credit cards until you have paid back your existing debts.

USE CASH.

Each week, take out a set amount of cash which is within your budget and covers your basic needs, such as food, petrol and other essential bills. Put your card where you cannot get at it.

Bills.

Revisit all your outgoings and see what you could save money on. You could switch your utility bills to a cheaper company and pay by direct debit, as most firms give you discount for doing so. Revise your home and car insurances and switch annually to save money. Your TV, broadband and phone should be evaluated to check if you can save money by switching or splitting providers.

Credit cards / Loans.

Switch your credit card or loan to providers with more favourable interest rates. One way to get rid of your card altogether is to switch to a Balance Transfer card, which will give you a 0% interest rate for a set time period. While you are in that time period, try to pay off the whole card. If you cannot manage that within the allocated period, look to another Balance Transfer.

Store cards.

Who has them anymore anyway? They charge the highest rates by far for any credit and they are the worst way to build up debt, so get rid of them now. Cut them up and start to pay them off. It's worth remembering that some bank accounts offer cash back in certain stores, so you can earn yourself money by using alternative ways of shopping.

Bank accounts.

Examine your current account and see what you are getting from it. Also look at the interest rates you are paying on your overdraft, or any payments you are making for added extras that you may not be using. There are numerous online bank accounts as well as the ones we know well, so shop around.

Savings.

If you have any savings, check the interest you are receiving. You could probably find better rates by switching to a new provider.

Mortgage.

The biggest expense you have each month is most likely to be your mortgage, so it is important that you get the best possible deal. It is always worth, in the first instance, going to your current mortgage lender to see what they can do for you, or going to see a financial adviser, who can scour the market to work out if it's worthwhile to switch.

Protection insurances.

It is worthwhile examining your insurances, such as your mortgage protection, critical-illness cover and income protection, as you could save money here. It may be that the policy you took out several years ago is no longer applicable to you, or you may be under-covered. A review will make sure you have adequate cover but you could also save some money if you have a savvy financial adviser who can hunt out the best products for you.

9

FINANCIAL MILESTONES/LIFE EVENTS

The Personal Financial Life Cycle. How does each stage of your life affect your personal finance choices?

What is the Personal Financial Life Cycle?

Traditionally, financial planning and tax planning have been carried out ad hoc throughout individuals' lives. We tend not to think about our financial strategy until something occurs where we need to scrutinise our spending. This usually happens when applying for a mortgage or making a Will. It seems that we purchase these products without any regard for what else we might need to complement them or how our lives will change in the future that could make them useless to us in one, five or 10 years down the road.

Most people follow a similar pattern with their personal finances. People should continuously refine and tweak their financial plans to meet their changing financial desires and needs. This becomes the life cycle.

WHY DO we need to think about it?

Each stage of our lives is influenced by many factors, including personal values, life choices, major life events and the needs of each physical stage of life. Some factors are expected, such as getting married or buying a house, and some are unexpected, such as redundancy or illness.

There are also a host of life conditions that are all relevant at different stages, including age, marital status, income, education, health, dependents and the economy. Some plans follow throughout our lives, such as savings or a mortgage, others are more critical at specific stages, such as making a Will once you have children.

Creating and following a life cycle plan gives you a better understanding of the rise of financial risk over time and what you will need to think about at set periods in your life. It establishes a way in which you can manage all your finances together, allowing you perhaps to finish paying off your mortgage early because you deliberately set up a savings plan or you bought investments that gave you the ability to pay for your children's education or their first property.

How to manage your wealth over time.

Within this life cycle, there are three basic stages of wealth – protection, accumulation and distribution:

- **Wealth Protection – 18 years to 45 years**

This is where you should be building financial security for your life ahead, doing cash management by setting goals about your career, lifestyle and family commitments. You need to do credit and debt management to avoid getting into too much debt, to protect yourself against economic downturns and to insure yourself in case you were suddenly to have an accident, for example.

- **Wealth Accumulation – 35 years to 64 years.**

This is where you have reached your peak in earning terms and are building your nest egg for your children's future and your retirement.

- **Wealth Distribution – 65-plus years.**

This is where you are spending your savings and pension during retirement and also planning what you are going to give to your loved ones when you pass away. These three stages give you an overview of how your money grows and falls throughout your life and helps you see where you may need to tighten up on your spending.

Sub Section 1: STAGE 1 & 2 – 11 to 24.

What are the stages of the financial life cycle?

The financial life cycle is split into six stages, each one with its own set of challenges and decisions.

The first stage is childhood, from age 11 years to 18 years.

All finances are the responsibility of your parents or carers at least up until 16 years old and you do not have to worry about where the next penny is coming in from until you start making choices about your career and what type of lifestyle you envisage for yourself. This is where parents can help by teaching kids the realistic value of money and what they need to do to achieve the goals they have set.

Parents can help their children by taking them into the bank or building society and opening a savings account with them. They can show them that having a job, such as a paper round or doing chores at home, can earn money to put into this account and grow the fund so it can pay for, perhaps, a large item they are longing for.

Children can also have a book in which to enter their receipts and keep a record of jobs/chores carried out plus the money earned. This can help reinforce good financial record keeping for the future, especially if they have to do their own tax returns eventually.

Talking about money and how much items cost can help children with their career path decisions. It is important to have open and honest discussions with youngsters about money as it will provide the knowledge about what they need to save for in the future and what will drain their income, such as property and children. This is especially important if they have an ideal style of life they want to keep. They may need to go to university, so saving for those fees will become crucial, or if they are learning while working, saving for a car may be more important.

Get kids learning through experiences as early as possible to build on this as they get older. Reward charts are a good place to start for younger children, earning money from doing chores will help the whole family.

THE SECOND STAGE is the young adult, 18 years to 24 years.

There are a lot of factors influencing your finances right now. This is a time of rapid personal growth as you become independent from your parents and start your journey through life.

If you are at university, the challenges will be how to make the most of the little money you have, and if you have a student loan, you need to maximise the use of that money so that you do not have to borrow further.

If you have decided to go straight into a job, you can start to save. This is the time to think about what you want from your career and where your aspirations lie. On-the-job training is a bonus as you do not have to pay for it, however if you want a specific career and your job is not in that field, you may have to finance your training yourself.

You may need to buy a car, so saving for that is vital, it can be tempting to take out car finance, however remember, a car is not an asset and it reduces in value. The interest you are paying never stops if you have a balloon payment or need to return the car. Maybe you would like to get your feet on the property ladder, meaning you will need to curtail your spending as saving for a mortgage can be a momentous task. It can feel like a time to spend and have no limits on that spending, but being a tiny bit sensible will hold you in a good stead long term.

You have to spend to accumulate. This works in different ways. In order to build a good credit rating, you need to take out some credit, such as a credit card or bank loan and prove that you can use it and pay it back within the schedule. The first thing you can do to help your credit rating is make sure you are on the electoral register even if you live with your parents or are at university... and you can do this as soon as you turn 18.

If you wish to buy a car or purchase a house, you will need to think about all the insurances and other associated payments, so you need to make sure that you have money in the bank throughout the month to pay these premiums.

It is worth getting some good solid financial advice at this stage. It will help you plan your financial future well and will also open your eyes as to what you will need to think about as you get older, such as starting a pension now will give you a much bigger retirement pot than if you were to wait until you are in your 30s. Now is the time to save, save, save.

Starting Out – Meet Amy:

Amy is a first-time buyer; she has been renting previously but returned home for a year to save a deposit to buy her first house. She has saved £10,000 and her parents have given her another £15,000 towards the purchase.

Amy works full time as a marketing manager. She loves her job but does not enjoy the commute into London. She would love to buy in London however house prices are just too high and outside her purchasing power.

Amy had considered buying with her boyfriend but she is concerned about her deposit and the money her parents have given her being passed on to him if they separated or if Amy was to pass away. She has learnt from the newspapers and television in the past seven years that, as a first-time buyer, she needed to have little or no debt in place to purchase her first home, that having credit cards and loans was not a good idea. Therefore, she has a low credit score from her credit file due to having only a £500 bank overdraft.

Thoughts to consider:

Amy could look at buying with her boyfriend and protect her £25,000 legally by writing a Will or by instructing the conveyancing solicitor to put in place trust paperwork that will ensure the money is returned to Amy should she split up from her boyfriend, forcing the house to be sold. This may allow her to buy closer into London, in a location she is happier living. Also, it may reduce the travel costs into London.

Subject to credit score lending, Amy could consider building up her credit file. This can be done in several ways but can take time, which in an upward market, means she could end up paying more for the same house in six months' times. One way to build her credit file would be to speak to her bank about a credit card and use it once a month for a small purchase but then clear if off each month. Ensuring she is placed on the Electoral Roll at her parents' address is also very important.

Predicting your own future is impossible. One thing that is certain is that you will face lots of change.

The lives and careers of women starting out today are very different from their parents' time. There are risks of persistent unemployment, climate change and continuous technological innovation.

You will be healthier and live for longer than your parents. Between education and retirement, you could have a 50-year career.

Your career will not be static.

Your employment is likely to involve different working patterns, different employers, different sectors, maybe even different countries. You may need to learn new skills along the way, and you may be surprised by the course down which your career takes you.

You may want to marry and start a family; but that does not mean you have to compromise on being financially, socially and spiritually independent.

My advice.

Do not enter this phase of your life without knowing your options. Develop skills and learn to strive for financial independence.

According to figures published last year by the National Insolvency Service, while the number of bankruptcies overall is down in England and Wales, young women are now more likely to fall into personal insolvency or bankruptcy than men. The gender gap is particularly noticeable when it comes to young adults, with 22.2 of every 10,000 women aged between 25 and 34 applying for bankruptcy or another insolvency status, compared with 21.2 of men the same age. This is the first time that the number of women applying for debt relief has overtaken men.

Sub Section 2: STAGE 3 – 25 to 34 years old.

If you have been to university, this is the start of your working life. If you have been working already, you will be in the throes of building your skill base to improve your career. It is in the early days, however, when you need to be aware of the financial risks that you may be taking, such as getting a mortgage, having children and keeping your health.

On the plus side, you have a fairly long period of working years ahead, so your ability to earn is seen as low risk. However, mortgages and children come with a higher risk. What is the risk? Well, what if something happens to you that could stop you from working and therefore stop you from bringing money into the household? How would you afford the mortgage payments and feed the children? These are factors that have to be taken into consideration when you look at mortgage payment protection, critical illness protection or income protection. All these insurances will help you, but they also incur a cost, which you need to plan into your monthly budget.

It is worth establishing a fund of about between three to six months' worth of your monthly salary as an emergency fund so that you have something to fall back on. It is normally at this stage that the need for credit is at its highest and managing this well will stand you in good stead as you get older. If you can save, it is also worth creating a fund for any children you have, whether it is for their education or for when they want to buy their first house or get married.

Long-term investment now will give them a bigger nest egg when they turn 18 or 21.

The age of new mothers is rising, however this is still the most common age to have children in the UK, and so there are several things you need to consider in advance of their arrival, such as reduced income while you are on parental leave, purchasing all the things that come with a baby and also life insurance should the worst happen once you are a parent. Taking into account childcare costs is a massive consideration. Often, women or parents are left with two options: stop working, as it is not viable due to the price of child care; or accept the costs and remain in your career until the child reaches three, when you start to get child-care assistance.

Once you have children, you should think about writing a Will, not just so that they will be financially secure if both parents should die, but also to establish who would look after the youngsters if they were to lose both parents. You do not want to leave it to the State to sort out. It is worth making sure they will be cared for by the people you trust, so a well-written Will is essential.

WORKING WOMAN – **Meet Zara.**

Zara has been married to Richard for four years. They brought their first home 10 years ago and moved to a larger house six years ago. The move and the wedding expenses were high and this has meant they are paying for a mortgage and paying for credit cards they have not managed to clear.

They feel they are paying out too much each month and are unable to save. They feel they do not have a handle on their finances and want to start getting ahead.

They have equity in their current home and they wonder if it would be worth clearing the credit cards with a mortgage instead.

Thoughts to consider:

The first thing to do is for them both to list what credit cards they have. Listing the company, the interest rate (not what it would be if they made a purchase), when that rate runs out and what it will revert to, what they are paying each month and if it is the minimum payment or not, what is the minimum payment percentage (usually 3% to 5% of the balance), what is the credit limit, and what the company might offer as a balance transfer rate and if there is a transfer fee.

Once Zara and Richard know this information, they will be able to see which credit cards are on a zero rate or a higher rate. The aim should be to have as much of the credit cards on zero per cent without paying any or much of a transfer fee. They may need to make a calendar note of when offers are available from and make a note of when any rates finish. Once they know how much total debt needs clearing, I would usually suggest they divide the total by either 12, 24, 36 or 48 months, giving them a monthly amount to pay back and a time to clear all the debt within. The monthly amount needs to be afford-able, however, as it is an over payment. And if one month they need to reduce it, they can do.

It is often advisable to clear this debt over a longer period, say five years, with their credit card providers on 0% interest rather than clearing the debt with a mortgage and paying the debt back over an even longer period, often 20 to 35 years. By doing this, you are paying more interest overall.

I would then like to see Richard and Zara's other spending to calculate if they are able to either clear the debts sooner or start saving towards back-up/emergency funds. We would usually like to see clients not have debts in place and making long-term saving plans. However, it would depend on individual circum-stances.

If you have a successful career and you are finally making the money you deserve, do you think about how you are going to make that money last?

It is time to consider turning surplus cash into savings that can start working for you, not just in the immediate term but for your future, too. One day you will want to step away from your business or job for good – invested savings will make that a reality.

MY ADVICE.

Do not be passive. Every phase of your life can be controlled by you when you create options for yourself. You can develop the skills, mentality and financial independence. I will help you to get them and to keep them.

You should not be afraid or intimidated to invest your savings. At Evolution Financial Planning, we make sure investing is not scary and help you to plan for life after work without using impenetrable jargon.

But the truth is, in order to build the wealth you want for your retirement, travel plans or trusts (investments) for your children, you need to invest. Once you start investing, you will find it is not as hard as you think.

Starting a family – Meet Claire.

Claire is a mum of three, with two of her children at school and one at nursery. She struggles to keep up with all the family commitments and the pressure of being a mother. Her partner is dad to one of the children and he works long hours. Claire manages all the household and financial bills per month but wonders what else she could do to support the family. She has been looking for part-time jobs to build up her own financial pot because when she separated from her first partner, she was left without many career options due to looking after the children.

Thoughts to consider:

Without taking benefits into account, as this would affect what she can claim, if she is already, Claire may want to consider some basic savings plans, such as an ISA, to put away as much of her own salary as possible. She is unlikely to have a pension or long-term savings in place so starting to get into the habit of saving a little would be important. Often, mothers find more ways to spend any additional income on the children. Claire needs to consider her longer term financial requirements, not just the immediate demands of the children.

Families have a long list of financial needs they should consider, from writing their Wills to ensuring that, should anything happen to the child's respective parent or care-giver, a plan is in place financially to look after that child. Life cover is the most obvious, however, there are several ways this can be put in place. They should also consider a trust for this policy.

With the joy of starting a family, having your first child marks the start of the most significant financial change of your life, that will last for the next 20 years.

A recent study by the Centre for Economics and Business Research found a typical parent can expect to spend £231,843 raising a child born in 2016. That's an increase of 65% since 2003. Imagine how that will change over the next 12 years.

The average UK parent will spend more than a third of their take-home pay just to be able to afford one child, with the costs highest between the ages of one and four years old.

In a child's first year, parents will spend £11,498, rising to £63,224, between one and four.

Being a mum today will be very different to the experiences of our mothers and grandmothers. Being healthier and living for longer than your parents means your finances will have to support you and your family for longer.

My advice.

Do not enter this phase of your life without any options. Have the skills, have the mentality, and have the financial independence.

Saving for your future should start today, as your finances will be stretched like never before. You will also want to protect your home if you are unable to pay your mortgage, and all the other important financial expenditures in life.

I know these may be the last things you want to think about when you are about to take a positive step in your life, but now can be the best time to consider your financial plan, for you and your new family.

ENTREPRENEURS – Meet Charmayne.

Charmayne started her company a year ago as a business consultant/coach. After many years working in the city for corporate clients, she felt she could help smaller business owners, work less hours and work on her own terms more.

Her income in the first year was slow to get started but she is beginning to see progress with a regular amount of client bookings each month, creating a regular cash flow. She manages all her money in one bank account and struggles to see what actual spare cash she has each month. Therefore, knowing what she can spend on herself or spend on her business is impossible.

Charmayne wants to develop her business online, creating a passive income with online courses and is looking at writing her first book, giving her creditability and also an additional revenue.

Thoughts to consider:

Charmayne needs to open a separate business or sole trader account for all her business revenue to go into. She needs to create a list of outgoings for that account and allow for any annual or future costs she foresees paying, such as marketing. Separately, we would usually suggest Charmayne lists her personal outgoings also, giving a monthly total. Ideally, the two totals should be the initial goal for invoicing clients each month. Ensuring she is strict with terms and conditions for payment – that is, settlement within 14 days or the end of the month, thus giving her three working weeks ahead to have the money in the account. Working with her money ahead of herself will allow Charmayne to stress less about her money and focus more on clients. When the money hits the account, Charmayne should pay herself FIRST, before anyone or anything else. Eventually, as she creates more clients, she can increase the amount she is paying herself. As soon as she is able, she should consider her pension needs, either as a sole trader or as she might progress into a limited company. It is easy to find more things to spend the revenue on in the business, "reinvesting back in the businesses", however the best thing your business can do for you is pay for your retirement first.

Having a bookkeeper or book-keeping system linked to her bank account will allow her to manage her money more easily and establish a better understanding of what money is hers to spend or invest.

More women are becoming entrepreneurs. We are choosing to create a legacy from our hard work, not just settle for earning a living. Women entrepreneurs can be any age. You may be right out of university, you may have an MBA, professional qualifications or simply be brilliant at what you do.

Our clients are women in their forties and fifties who want to explore a different career and discover their passion.

To be a female entrepreneur means becoming someone who is discovering your ability of endurance and developing the crucial belief system on your way to success.

MY ADVICE if you are starting out as an entrepreneur.

Get your concept right, from initial sales and testing. Know what you can charge and make sure you possess sufficient confidence to not be overshadowed or under appreciated by anyone.

Running your own business is a journey of self-discovery. You may have heard that from other people, or read it. Well, it is not a cliché; it is reality.

Those more established.

Try not to fall into the trap of spending everything and your business becoming the bank of all things. It should be used as an asset creating tool to enable your future.

Sub Section 3: STAGE 4– 35 to 52 years old.

This stage is seen as your later working years. It is characterised by the fact that you may have more than one child, your children may be at school and you may be caring for elderly parents.

The financial challenges at this stage of life are more complicated as you may want to help your children pay for their university fees or assist them with a deposit on their first property. Both of these are sizable expenditures so it is worth planning for these as early as you can to build up a decent amount of money by the time it is needed. If you have more than one child, there should be a pot for each, ideally.

This is also the time when you need to think about protecting your income in case of injury or illness. A health issue could knock your lifetime savings if you do not have cover and you may not be able to pay the mortgage or the bills. This could have devastating effects on your family and home. It is this stage where most claims are made. According to a report by Legal & General, the average age for critical illness claims is 45 years old and the average age for terminal illness claims is 55 years.

It is worth looking at and revising your pension now. You need to understand how much money you will need for your retirement and the number of years that you can work is reducing, so it is crucial that you can put as much as you can into your pension now.

This is also a time where people re-evaluate their careers or decide that they want to retrain. There is a requirement for more income as the family has more financial needs. Re-training has both cost and time obligations, so it is worth having some savings in the pot before you quit your full-time job.

It is also at this stage where a lot of people are caring for their parents, whether it is just their finances or whether they have to move them into a home. There are financial obligations to be met here and it is worth getting sound financial advice in order to maximise assets and ensure that healthcare needs are met.

Returning to work – Meet Suzie.

Suzie has been a 'stay at home' mum for 15 years, having previously she worked in a school as an office manager. Now her children are older and do not need her attention so much, she is wanting to work 25 hours a week to give herself more spare money each month and to pay for bigger holidays for the family.

The family's earnings would normally go into a joint account but she wants to keep this income separate and pay for some of the bills.

Suzie is unsure what she should be considering financially at this stage of life.

Thoughts to consider.

A suggestion would be for her to work out her total net income (what she would be paid each month into her bank account) and that of her partner and to calculate the key family outgoings. For example:

Her income is £850 and her partner is £1,850, giving a joint income of £2,700, while their outgoings are £1,200 per month. She brings home 31.5% of their combined income and he earns the other 68.5%. Therefore, to pay a share of their outgoings equal to their earnings, Suzie would pay £378 and her partner would pay £822.

Depending on how her partner feels about this level of income from her, they may decide to focus her salary on just saving for the family holidays. We would normally suggest the holiday package is priced up and divided by the number of months before the bill needs to be paid, thus giving you a monthly amount to put aside.

However, Suzie also needs to consider her pension options as she has not been contributing to one for 15 years and needs to think about what her plans would be, once she and her partner do retire.

Returning to work is a personal issue. Many mums would love to stay home but it is not financially feasible for everyone to do so. Others simply do not want to stay at home for various reasons.

If you have a successful career and you are getting ready to return to work after pregnancy, the first thing to understand is there is never a perfect time. Just like when you started your family in the first place, there is never a 'right' time to go back.

Putting aside the financial benefits of returning and the impact of being at home, returning to work is a big emotional step. *I know this from my own experience.*

My advice.

You need to take control of the situation. Every phase of your life can be controlled by you when you create space for yourself. The space comes from developing the skills, mentality and financial independence.

Communication about money in relationships can be a formidable issue.

Now is the time to talk about the financial goals you and your partner share. Discussing what is important in life involves your budget: debts, cash management, emergency funds, insurance protection, retirement savings and more.

Having a double income contributing to the family home can make things seem rosy, but it all changes when childcare costs come along. It means an added risk if one of you loses your job or becomes ill. Establish what needs to be covered in an emergency and build your plan.

One in five UK adults has experienced economic abuse by a current or former partner.

What is economic abuse?

This relates to financial abuse plus restricting, exploiting, or sabotaging other resources, such as housing, food, property, transportation and employment.

Both these sorts of abuses can develop slowly and could begin with behaviour that at first seems protective or caring, for example, offering to take care of the all the finances or encouraging you not to work so that you can look after the children.

What is financial abuse?

This is defined as someone controlling a person's access to their finances, hindering a person's ability to earn, stealing money or coercing someone into debt. All of these reduce a person's independence.

Surviving economic abuse.

Many women experience economic abuse within the context of intimate partner violence. It limits their choices and ability to access safety.

Surviving Economic Abuse and Women's Aid are two charities that help women in these circumstances. It is a complex and delicate area and needs to be tackled carefully.

www.survivingeconomicabuse.org

www.womensaid.org.uk

Sub Section 4: STAGE 5 – 55 to 64.

This is the period in which you are heading towards retirement. A review of your pension is a must. You have fewer years to work and therefore, fewer years to save for your retirement. You need to look at what income you will have for your retirement years and whether you will have enough to last you.

It is worth looking at what you have in savings and investments at this point and seeing if you are able to make more out of them in the next 10 years. It may be that you need to, or wish to, carry on working after you retire from your current career and do some part-time work or voluntary work to keep you active.

You may want to help your children with their first home or wedding costs; however, these are very large purchases and you may need to dip into your savings or other assets to help them out. Is this going to affect their inheritance or your lifestyle when you retire?

You may want to re-evaluate your property and whether it is too big for your needs or whether you wish to be closer to your children, or even emigrate. You may be able to save money by downsizing or living somewhere less expensive. Also, take into account that a smaller home will come with cheaper energy bills and lower council tax.

However, if you do not want to move because you are already close to your children, there are equity release schemes available. Most schemes allow you to borrow money using your home as the security. In essence, you are lending some of your home's value to a company and the scheme will get their money back when your house is sold, more often than not at your death, or if you go into a nursing home.

There are different types of equity release schemes and it is worth researching them before you make your decision. Remember, you will be reducing the amount that you will be leaving to your family in your Will and such schemes can be expensive to buy. Talk to a financial adviser to make sure that you have looked at all the implications that doing this may have on your financial circumstances.

It is important to make sure that your Will is still valid and relevant. A review is always a great idea as there may be grandchildren who you did not have when you wrote it. You may have decided to help one child out financially and want to leave more of your remaining assets to the other(s) to compensate. But if it's not written down, it may not be sorted out that way once you are gone, so it is better to get it done now. Also consider, if you have not already, having your lasting power of attorney for health and welfare plus property and financial affairs. You can do this yourself via the Office of the Public Guardian if you feel able or you can enlist a professional Will writer or solicitor to do it for you.

Whatever you decide, make sure you: seek advice; can pay back any money you may borrow; and you are not giving your children a debt that they cannot repay once you have gone.

Empty Nest

I often think there is no starker contrast between my generation and my mother's than when it is time for our children to leave home.

My friends and I, if we did not go to university, left home in our early twenties, as early as possible for some of my friends. Yet today, for various financial reasons, children are leaving home much later and are likely to return home after university.

When it does happen, it is an emotional event, just like returning to work. Some of my clients tell me that they did not know whether to jump up and down with excitement or curl up into a ball and cry.

When your children were at home, your life probably revolved around them. Even older children require practical and emotional support. Now your life is entering a new phase and it is time for you to become an empty-nester.

My advice.

Following some reflection, start planning. Every phase of your life can be controlled by you, when you see the possibilities. The possibility to do what you want comes from developing the skills, mentality and financial independence.

Permit yourself to turn your spare cash into savings that can work for you in retirement.

Investing may seem scary and you probably want to make sure you have enough in case anything goes wrong. Well, you can probably protect yourself and still save for your future. It is a case of creating a financial plan that enables you to do both.

The truth is that you can afford to focus on you now. It's your time.

Getting divorced.

Meet Deborah, she has been married for 21 years and has recently filed for divorce. Her ex-partner and herself have two children, aged 12 and 14. She has met with her lawyer but is really at the start of the process and is unsure what will happen and what needs to be looked at. Her partner has dealt with the main finances, however, she looked after day-to-day expenses, such as the food. She feels ready to understand her new financial future and get into a new strong position.

She plans to continue working part time at the local primary school and wants to retain the family home, so her children do not have to move schools. However, she will not be able to maintain the property or the mortgage on her own with her salary. This is her primary concern.

Thoughts to consider:

The first thing for Deborah to do would be to ensure she has collected as much paperwork as possible. Her lawyer will need to understand all her debts, assets, income and outgoings at the current property. Her ex-partner will need to do the same for negotiations to start.

Mortgage wise, the lender will take into consideration benefits and court maintenance so Deborah should get a mortgage capacity letter from a broker or mortgage provider to show her lawyer the affordable mortgage options available to her.

The valuation of the property and any assets, such as pensions, are taken into account when it comes to maintenance, short or long term. It is key that Deborah puts herself in a good position so that the mortgage is covered as well as her bills and day-to-day living costs.

No one plans to get divorced when they get married but it still happens to around 42% of couples in the UK, according to the Office for National Statistics. And that number may be rising.

Even if you have seen it coming for some time, it is normal to feel numb. Working through the practicalities that your decision involves can feel overwhelming.

You may be feeling powerless and angry about what has happened if you had not wanted the relationship to end, compounded with a sense of loss and sadness.

This is a time when you need to get the support and advice of other people. You might also find it helpful to write down all the things you have to deal with now your life is entering a new phase.

My advice.

Make some time for yourself. By the conclusion of the whole process, you will be feeling worn out. You might have had to change jobs or houses and your financial position would have most definitely have changed. Following some reflection, you should consider what you want to do next. Every phase of your life can be controlled by you when you see the possibilities. The ability to do what you want comes from developing the skills, mentality and financial independence. You may want to think about a new career or take up several new hobbies. The truth is that you can afford to focus on you now. It is your time. Depending on where this leaves you will dictate your next financial plan.

Sub Section 5: STAGE 6 – 65 years plus.

Scottish Widows report found that 71% of women do not know what pension pot they need to secure a retirement income they hope for... but 52% of women are saving adequately for retirement.

If you have not already, this is the time people think about downsizing, moving closer to their children or other family members or even emigrating. Depending on your retirement income and your health, it is worth working out how much you have in the pot and what you will need annually to give you the lifestyle that you would like.

Look at your insurances, as they rise quickly once you retire and you may not have adequate cover for your needs. Re-evaluate what you need them for and whether the plans you have in place are relevant to you now. It is worth seeking advice to make sure that you are covered correctly. Also ensure that your Will is up to date and relevant as your situation or that of your children may have changed.

This is the time, while you are still fit and healthy and of sound mind, to speak to an adviser and your family to arrange a Lasting Power of Attorney (LPA) for your financial affairs. It will allow someone you trust to look after your assets if you should become too unwell to handle this. You can also do this for health decisions so that someone can talk to your doctor on your behalf. If you have not put this in place, your family may have to go to court to be granted this power to help you, otherwise your family will have no control over where you should receive your care and how it is funded. You can find more information about this here:

www.gov.uk/government/organisations/office-of-the-public-guardian

Lastly, make sure that you are claiming all the state benefits that you may be entitled to. There are many people who think they do not qualify and are missing out on that useful extra cash at this time in their lives.

Retiring – meet Mary:

Mary has paid into a few different company pensions for many years. She is 50 and wishes to retire at age 65. She earns £27,500 per year as a researcher for a charity. She contributes 5% of her salary currently (£114 per month) and her employer matches it. This could mean her pension pot at age 65 would be £151,865. At age 65, she would be able to draw a cash-free lump sum of up to 25% (£37,996) with the remaining funds providing an income of £5,722 per year - £476 per month. Most people would like to see a retirement income of at least around 70% of their current annual salary

10 Ways to Accelerate Your Wealth

to live a comfortable lifestyle. In this example, she would be £690 a month short of this.

Her state pension would not start until age 67 and is currently £155.65 per week.

We're all living longer, especially women. That means you will most likely have more time to enjoy your retirement.

But living longer also means you have a greater chance of outliving whatever you have saved. In fact, this is often considered the number one financial worry for most women.

To compound it, while my peers and my daughter's generation in particular, have benefitted from gender equality, you are still at a disadvantage when it comes to accumulating money for your retirement. The reality is that you will need to save more to live comfortably in retirement.

My advice.

Do not enter this phase of your life without options. Have the skills, have the mentality, and have the financial independence for a long and contented retirement. I will help you have them and keep them.

Consider how you can turn as much of your spare cash into savings that can work for you in retirement.

Investing may seem risky and you probably want to make sure you have enough for a rainy day. Creating a financial plan enables you to do both. Protect yourself and still secure your future savings.

This has given you snapshots of the various stages in your life with regards to your finances. I would like to think it has helped provide a valuable insight into what financial products you need to set up at particular times in order to make life run that bit more smoothly as you get older. By looking at the life cycle process, you will be able to re-evaluate your plans over time to ensure that you have the correct savings, insurance and investments at each stage. You will be able to minimise your spending and control your debt to help yourself live the life you really want.

Which stage are you at in life and what is coming up you might need to plan for?

10

THE MONEY MATRIX™

Once you have established the foundation of your money, you establish what you want for your own personal perspective, you will know what you spend your money on each month, you will appreciate how much you have spare and how much you can afford to save.

So, the rest is easy, right? This is where it gets more interesting.

This chapter will explore how you start to align your finances to the areas that need your attention, give them purpose and then, with the processes in place, watch it all come together with ease.

STEP 1: Goals and Vision.

As we have discussed in previous chapters, putting value on why you created these new habits is one of the main key elements to success. Doing it for the sake of it is not enough. We are driven by two things: either avoiding pain or gaining pleasure.

With the Money Makeover Programme exercise, we looked at 10 key personal values:

- Creativity/personal expression,
- Professional development,
- Growth of self,
- Family,
- Relationships,
- Health,
- Independence,
- Personal legacy,
- Sense of control,
- Security.

What where your top five values?

What areas of your life need some focus?

Where do you need to start focusing your money - maybe reduce other spending and give your money a job - to start to create the life you want?

What do you want your life to look like short, medium and long term? By the time you're 20, 30, 40, 50, 60, 70 and 80 plus, what do you want your life to look and feel like?

Sometimes, it is easier to say what you do not want your life to look like, however try to focus on the positive things rather than the negatives.

What kinds of skills do you want to have? How do you want to be expressing yourself? In the garden? Speaking on stage? With animals? Around children?

What do you want your family relationships to look and feel like?

What do you want your intimate relationships to look and feel like?

How do you want your health to be?, How do you want your body to feel?

What kind of choices do you want to be able to make financially?

You should have a list of goals that you want to achieve now or in the future. Writing these down in a time-line is a great way to reflect back and check how you are getting on.

Vision boards are a great tool to put all those concepts into one place, too. To visualise these goals is not literally writing a list, but creating a vision of these elements of your life. They are not necessarily objects, such as a car or a boat or a house, but a feeling or a way of life. You can do this by collecting magazines or printing pictures from the internet. You start to compile images of those goals and you can either pin them on a board or stick them to pieces of paper. Some people do this with images via apps. The important point is that you spend time to find the right images. What you focus on is what you achieve. Having those images or pictures around you on a regular bases will help you feel keep that focus and not get distracted.

Ok, so now we need to prioritise five immediate top things that you could take some actions and shifts towards right now? What is something you need to action on urgently and give the most attention? What is critical, what is a need or what is a want?

Perhaps it will mean paying for a specialist evening class, building a deposit for your first home, going back to college or joining a gym.

Give your money a job, decide how and by when you want to achieve those goals and set an amount with a target date.

STEP 2: Cash Flow Allocation.

Practically speaking, you then need to break down those goals, with a realistic savings plan. Ideally, not all your monthly income will be spent on 'fixed or set expenditures' (mortgage or rent, insurances, food, child care). If you totalled all of yours, what percentage of your fixed or set expenditures is spent of your monthly salary? The aim would be that 50% of your income would go on fixed or set expenditures.

Other spending, 'essential/non-essential expenditures', it could be taking the kids out swimming or having a coffee or lunch out with friends, comes next.

If you put your essential/non-essential expenditures in play money, how much of a percentage is it of your monthly salary?

This is where you need to break down those essential/non-essential expenditures into values. How does your spending align to those values?

The aim would be to have 50% of your spending on fixed and set expenditures – the remaining 50% spent on your top five values. For example:

£2,500 per month total

£1,250 50% Necessities

£250 10% Financial freedom, personal pension or investments

£250 10% Long-term savings – for a holiday or new home

£250 10% Education – new course to learn a language

£25010% Play – eating out and kids' days out

£25010% Give/charity – animal protection league.

Total£2,500

Before you start to become a massive long-term investor, the starting point is to create some basic savings accounts in which to place the emergency funds and the personal 'goal' money. If that is a regular amount or just a fund to access, the easiest way to manage this is to ring-fence the money to ensure that it cannot be accessed daily. You must be sure the monies are not included in your monthly outgoings for bills. Some banks will allow you to have several accounts and even 'name' them. Alternatively, you can keep a spread sheet for your reference.

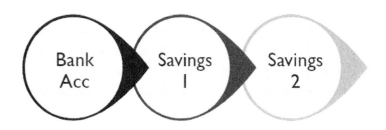

And here is your fifth of 10 ways to accelerate your wealth –

Number 5:

Give your money a job. Have the money going to 'spaces' or 'pots' where you have named the pot/space and have a clear goal of what it is your using that money for. Holiday, new car, days out, treat myself pot… etc.

Try not to do too much at once, prioritise your top critical goals. If that means using a certain amount from another goal, which you might need to put off for a while, then do it.

Live your life in aligned wealth rather than random and haphazard spending.

STEP 3: What are you worth?

Take a moment to work out what you are worth right now, and then up until your retirement age, without increasing your salary. Take your annual salary or, if you wish, the household annual salary, multiply this by the time until your retirement.

- Your retirement age – let's use 66 years old (though it might be older) minus your current age.

For example: £20,000 per year for the household

- 30 years old now take away 66 = 36 years

36 years x £20,000 = £720,000.00

You are your own cash machine. That is a lot of money, and when we work it out like that, it really shows us how much we all must waste.

How you spend your time making and spending money matters.

STEP 4: 10% to 20% investing.

Ideally, once someone has enough earnings, spending should not increase in line with that but instead increase the investing allocation.

If individuals can start to use 10% to 20% for investing either in pensions or investments or an asset that grows or provides returns, this is how we start to shift our wealth from lack mindset and 2D to a wealth mindset and 3D. Even if you can start with only 5%, it's a start.

These simple images represent how most people spend their money.

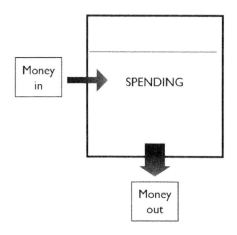

The larger box represents your main bank account, with money coming in each month. The arrow going down/out is your money going out each month with your spending. The arrow going in is your money coming into your account. Above the line is spare money. However, this is often spent also, some might be put into savings for emergency. Little is invested.

We have grown up in an age of spending, buying what we want, when we want it - not *need* but *want*. The process continues by taking out more finance to fund this spending need. We do not save for a car; we get a loan and inadvertently invest nothing for our future.

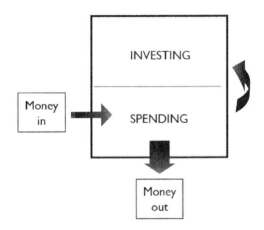

The smart way of managing finances is to create an income from income. Use your initial income and put efforts into investing or saving. Creating an income to spend will produce longer term benefits. Passive income is very much what many people will be looking for in the future. In fact, they have had to get educated and smart with money.

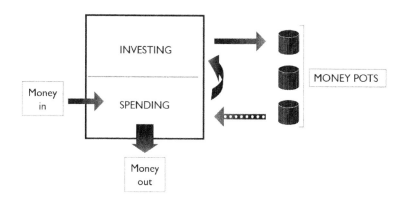

The arrow represents revenue return or income money coming in. As this increases, providing you with more money to play with at a later stage when you need it, you can achieve your personal value goals and create more income to be invested. This is how those with money seem to have it easier.

And here is your sixth of 10 ways to accelerate your wealth −

Number 6:

Set up at least one wealth pot; that might be a pension, S&S ISA, a property rental, angel investment, a bond − there is a long list of different ways. Once you have one, you can continue to build the different pots and allow them to grow. Then later in life, turn that money into an income, allowing you to retire early or stop work completely.

Be sure to choose something which is safe and regulated - there are many scams out there. I will be covering the more traditional assets in the next few paragraphs. An asset will give you a return in income or revenue either to use now or to reinvest again to create the compound effect.

Things to consider:

Compound Interest.

As mathematical genius Albert Einstein once said: *"Compound interest is the eighth wonder of the world. He who understands it, earns it. He who doesn't, pays it."*

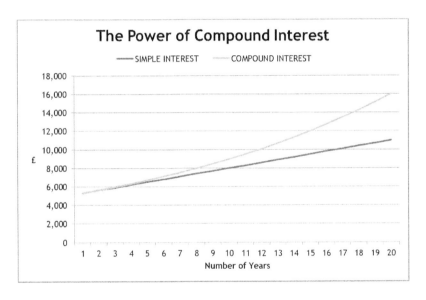

This is where the interest you earn on your savings or investments is added to the initial investment pot... and you then earn interest on the interest. As the graph shows, this increases your overall investment or monies earned. In this example, we highlight how an investment of approximately £5,800 would provide the client with a return of approximately £11,000, a £5,200 profit with simple interest (the red line) – almost doubled the money over 20 years. With compound interest (the green line) – that is interest on the interest – the return would be £16,000, an additional £5,000.

What is 'Inflation?'

Inflation is the rate at which the general level of prices for goods and services is rising and, consequently, the purchasing power of currency is falling. Central banks attempt to limit inflation, and avoid deflation, in order to keep the economy running smoothly.

Therefore, if all your savings are sitting in a standard bank account or savings account with an interest rate lower than the rate of inflation, your money is losing value. The rate of interest should be higher, at the very least, than the rate of inflation. This is an issue to those relying on savings to provide an income when interest rates are low.

Debts and mortgages.

I have already mentioned that it is important to have an emergency pot of at least three times income. This is to ensure you do not have to use credit (loans and credit cards) to purchase items, therefore creating debts. Even if the credit card is at 0%, at some point this will run out... and when you want to transfer it to another facility, you could be charged a transfer fee. This is also a monthly commitment, even if it is a minimum payment, it is an amount that you are spending that cannot be invested.

Loans have their initial interest and fees added right from the start, before you even make a payment. Then, the total debt is repaid over a period of months or years. Again, this is a monthly commitment and you are paying back interest as well as the debt itself. If you can save and pay for the item outright, this is better in the long term.

A mortgage is quite possibly the biggest debt that an individual may have in their lifetime. Here is an example of how much you are paying back, even with a small loan of £97,500 over 25 years and a low interest rate of 2.74% for two years:

- With a two- year fixed interest rate of 2.74% that will revert to Standard Variable Rate, 4.50% in two years, for the remaining term of the mortgage, the total amount to be reimbursed is £204,939.00

This means that you will pay back £2.10 for every £1 borrowed. Can you imagine if I lent you £100 but I asked for £210 back? When you put it like that, it makes you think. Your mortgage is not just £100 or, if you are lucky, it will not be £100,000 either. The quicker we pay back debts, the more this allows us to free up capital to invest and not be paying interest on it. The example below shows a repayment mortgage over 25 years with the client making over payments, thus reducing the debt and paying off the mortgage quicker - 10 years quicker.

Your mortgage debt over time

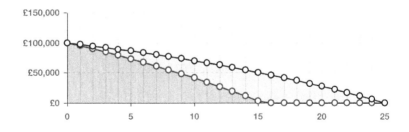

This illustrates how a £100,000 mortgage over 25 years, with overpayments of £500 a month, will save £82,772 in interest and reduce the term to just over 15 years.

You can see the importance of clearing debt. I should say, the highest rate of interest debts are an important part of your financial journey. Once you are out of the red and into the black, you can seriously consider where to save and how to invest.

IMPORTANT NOTE.

The decision to overpay on your mortgage or invest is a calculation that depends on expected investment rate of return, which will always be an assumption, and the expected rate of interest on the mortgage. Also, it is dictated by the size of the mortgage and how much could be invested monthly or as a lump sum. By running the comparisons, this will reveal whether you should invest all the money or overpay the mortgage.

Priority to have the mortgage cleared before retirement is usually a key factor for most clients.

11

FINANCIAL PRIORITIES PYRAMID

Now it is time to look at your financial priorities, the hierarchy for any financial plan starts with living for today – putting food on the table. As a financial planner, we have to ensure that clients are not placing their own or their family's basic living needs at risk. Unless a client has substantial wealth (as in millions of pounds), protection or insurance to pay for your basic living for today is next on the priorities. That is income to pay for those things, a pension for future retirement, savings and then investments.

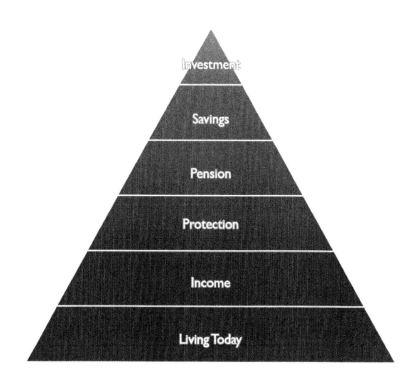

1. Living today.

Women make 85% of purchasing decisions and have significantly more control over the household finances than they had 10 years ago, a survey claimed.

Three-quarters of women said they thought they now had more control over the payment of domestic bills than a decade ago, according to the research by car giant Vauxhall. And 56% of men agreed with this.

At the same time, 61% of women in a relationship thought they had more say over savings accounts, while 51% of men thought their partner was now more involved in this aspect of their finances. But while the majority of women felt they now took overall control of the domestic finances, the majority of men still thought that they were in charge.

And while 54% of men claimed they took care of domestic bills, only 9% of women thought their partner took the lead in this area.

For this reason, the day-to-day purchasing power of women has increased and we have become great at finding the best deals to provide the family with living essentials. This is our basic human need. Of course, everyone has a different version of what is 'essential'.

Sources:

https://www.theguardian.com/women-in-leadership/2016/feb/03/how-advertising-industry-fails-women

http://www.manchestereveningnews.co.uk/business/property/women-hold-pursestrings-1023819

2. Income.

Income provides necessities for our families. Some people have the level of drive and determination to provide more, with women tending to spend additional money on anything apart from themselves.

The difference in the average salary between men and women, according to a government report, is 19.1%. For every £1 that men earn, women earn 80p. This is based on both full and part-time work.

The Office for National Statistics stated in its November 2014 survey that the gap is actually 9.4% based on full-time hours excluding overtime.

It says that, with regards to part-time work, this is reversed and it is actually women who earn more, 5%. However, this can be explained by the fact that women tend to work part time throughout their working life whereas men may work part time only at the beginning or end of their careers.

The Office for National Statistics report, 2020, states the gender pay gap among all employees was 15.5% in 2020, down from 17.4% in 2019.

Source:

ons.gov.uk/employmentandlabourmarket/peopleinwork/earningsandworkinghours/bulletins/genderpaygapintheuk/2020

Why do women earn less?

There are several reasons why women tend to earn less than men. For example:

- There are more women in lower paid jobs, such as healthcare where it is found that average wages are £40 less a week than the national average. This is where 80% of the workforce are women. There are fewer women managers, and when they do get to management, they are paid less than their male counterparts. Women dominate the workforce in childcare, 94%, and in secretarial positions, 92%, however, only 7% are engineers and 20% are architects, which are much higher paid positions.

Additionally, when weekly pay rates were researched, the gap was even bigger because men tend to work longer hours than women, they are more likely to do overtime and they receive bigger bonuses.

The gap varies in different industries. The Office for National Statistics found that in the transportation, mining, storage and quarrying sectors, women earn on average around 3% more than men. In finance, insurance, technical, scientific and utilities, men earn significantly more than women, on average around 27%.

3. Protection.

There are several different types of protection requirements. I find with clients that their perceived risk is actually not correct.

Life and critical illness insurance can be taken out for a particular sum assured and over a particular term required. Life insurance covers the person insured in the event of death while critical illness insurance covers the person insured on diagnosis of a defined critical illness.

Why would you have life and crucial illness insurance?

You would have this kind of insurance to cover a mortgage or a debt to ensure a continuation of the lifestyle that your family has become accustomed to, or provide income to care for young children until they are of adult age.

How do you know what level of critical illness you are getting?

There is a guide from Defaqto, an independent financial information business, that gives star ratings based on a selection of factors.

Each insurance company covers a certain amount of defined medical definitions, ranging from 25 to 166. Some of these definitions are what is referred to as ABI – Association of Business Insurers – meaning some of those particular definitions meet the ABI standard.

We do not like to think that anything bad will happen to ourselves or our families, however, according to the ABI study in September 2014, around a million people each year are forced to take time off work due to a serious illness or an injury.

Think about it. If you had to be absent from work because you had a serious illness or you had an injury which meant you could not do your job, how would you or your family cope with the loss of income? Your employer may have protection that will enable them to pay you sickness pay. However, this could be a fraction of your salary.

According to reports from leading human resources website, Personnel Today, just 12% of employers support their staff for more than one year if they are off sick. The Government's website says the minimum Statutory Sick Pay an employer has to provide after three continuous sick days is only £88.45 a week, for a maximum of 28 weeks.

How would you pay the monthly bills? Some people rely on government benefits, but will they be enough to cover your outgoings?

One way of approaching this is to take out Income Protection insurance. This is a long-term policy that will help you if you have a serious illness or injury. This starts after your sickness pay has stopped from your employer.

It is different to Critical Illness insurance, which pays out a lump sum if you have a specific illness. The Government's website states that most common causes for income protection claims are for illnesses that would not be covered under Critical Illness policies.

Income Protection.

You can get cover for one year, two years or until you retire. It replaces part of your income if you cannot work at all. It is based on a percentage of your salary, the usual amounts are 50% or 70% and payments are tax free.

It will pay out until you start working again or until the end of the policy, or you retire or, in the worst-case scenario, you pass away.

You have to wait a period of time before the payments start, called your deferred period, which is agreed when you take out the policy. It is usual that these payments do not start until your sick pay stops or other insurances cease to provide funds. The longer you have chosen the waiting time to be, the smaller your monthly policy payments will be. The normal time can be 4, 8, 13, 26 or 52 weeks.

This will cover most illnesses that leave you unable to work. You need to check the policies as they all differ. You can claim more than once from one policy while it is still valid.

It is worth checking with your employer before you apply for this insurance, just in case their sick pay would be more than enough for you to live on.

Think about the long term. Would your employer's sick pay cover your income for 12 months or more? If not, it is worth getting advice as to the best protection you can get for you and your family.

4. Pension.

Consider this: in 1900, the average life expectancy for a woman was just 50 years of age. Today, it is 81 years of age. Thanks to advances in living conditions, diet and medical care, we are all living longer – but few of us stop to think what impact this will have on our later lives.

According to a study by Public Health England published in April 2016, women aged under 65 are likely to spend almost a third of their lives in retirement, such is their future life expectancy.

This might sound like a blissful way to kick back and relax for a few decades, but it means most women will have to commit much more to their pension than they realise – or spend many years having to cut their cloth extremely tightly.

The amount you receive will depend on a number of factors – the age when you start paying in, the pension product you choose, your salary, and the size of employer contributions to your fund, to name a few examples.

There is a basic state pension available to those of retirement age, but it is minimal. The current maximum allowance available through a state pension is £119.30 per week. Most people choose to 'top it up' by contributing to a private pension scheme.

Even auto enrolment workplace schemes might not be sufficient to give you adequate retirement funds, with the required contributions in 2016 set very low.

The Office for National Statistics has revealed that just under 50% of people do not have a private pension. This means that when they retire, they will be relying on the State or any investments they have to fund their income.

Pension companies are struggling to fund individuals' retirements mainly due to an ageing population and low interest rates. Many schemes are in debt and others are generally under-performing. So, is it worth getting a private pension, or should we look to save our money another way?

Why bother?

About 12% of people surveyed by the ONS said that they wish they had never taken out a pension because it is under-performing and it will not provide enough income in their retirement.

Reuters revealed that many pension schemes are in deficit, which means that they do not have enough funds to pay out what they will finally owe to their pension holders when they retire.

Pensions money is invested in the stock market. Depending on how good your fund manager is dictates the size of your fund, which could even decrease if they make poor judgment in their investment choices, if their charges are high, or if the stock market struggles. These are risks we all take in order to give us a good pot of money when we retire.

You have the control, you can transfer your pension into a better performing one, you can change your broker and you have the power to decide what stocks and shares your money will go into.

You also cannot get to your money until retirement, so you have to wait before you can spend the money. This can be a good thing for some people who would be tempted to spend it before they retire and, therefore, leave themselves with nothing.

There are some amazing tax benefits of having a pension and everyone should have one.

What type of pension to have?

Private pensions mean that you have to fund them yourself, but it is a secure form of paying for your retirement and you have total control over who you choose as a fund manager and where your money is held.

Employer pensions have the possibility of your employer contributing towards it too, with some even matching what you are putting in, which is an added bonus. However, you do not have control over which company manages your funds.

All pensions are tax efficient, too. If your payments come straight from your gross salary, you will not pay tax on them. If they do not, you can claim back the tax.

A pension also provides security. It is a guaranteed income for the rest of your life once you retire.

Remember, it is worth starting early. Many young people going into their first job will not even think about pension contributions, but with longer living and the State not being able to provide, it is worth taking the step of starting your pension early to build up a decent fund. Who knows what will happen in 30 years' time, we may not even have a National Health Service to rely on.

A pension is still a very good way to save for your retirement and should be thought about as part of your investment strategy. It is worth getting solid advice before making a decision. A financial adviser can help you choose what is right for you.

5. Savings.

Saving versus investing: what's best?

When you are financially stable and ready to start planning for the future, you might want to consider long-term investing – for example, in a stocks and shares ISA alongside a standard savings account.

This can grow your nest egg more quickly than standard savings, but bear in mind that the value of investments can go down as well as up and you may not get back the amount you invested.

Depending on how bold you want to be, there are a number of risk profile options available, which a financial adviser can talk you through. A medium-risk investment might not have the same high returns as high risk, but it offers greater stability.

Being young, you also have the benefit of choosing a longer 'time horizon' for your investment. However, your investment plan should be mapped to your personal objectives. For example, if you are hoping to buy a house in two years, choose that as your 'time horizon', so you can cash in the money for a deposit when the right moment comes around.

Scottish Widows research revealed that human beings are focused, by nature, on the immediate, wanting satisfaction and fulfilment right now and having little interest in putting them off. In the world of finance, that means we want to see the guaranteed benefits of our money immediately instead of wondering about our future, which is intangible and delayed, even if we know that it means our lives in the future will be secure.

As a nation, how do we plan for the long-term future of our finances?

This is the question the Scottish Widows report was looking to answer. We do know that we must save for the future, but so many people ignore it or put it off. Their report is based on an online survey of 5,000 plus adults in the United Kingdom and was conducted in March 2014 by the independent research agency, YouGov. It asks about the attitudes to saving and how people can manage their money more efficiently.

Caroline Rookes, CEO of the Money Advice Service, says: "This report suggests that many people instinctively understand the need to cut back when the going gets tough. That's good news. It's not quite such a positive finding that, while people refuse to countenance reducing their phone or mobile usage, they find it comparatively easy to cut back on protecting their assets and their families against an unwelcome turn of events."

Around 19% of people in the UK have no savings at all. That doesn't sound like a big number until you put it into number of people, that is around 12.4 million, one quarter of the adult population.

There are 17.5 million people between the ages of 35 and 49 years old yet a massive 55% of those think that individuals should take more responsibility for saving more.

The average amount in savings per person during 2013 was £2,882.

When put under pressure, people will cut back on eating out, entertainment and more than half would stay in more often.

About 33% of us are saving proportionately more than we were two years ago but more than half are actually saving less.

More men (50%) than women (46%) said a preference for spending their money was a barrier to saving.

The report notes that many people are still not sure what long term means and how much we need to save to cover emergencies, holidays and our retirement. Everyone wants to retire early but they still want to spend money now rather than thinking about putting it away for the future.

6. Investments.

Investments are a great way of making your money work well for you. In the economic climate where interest rates are very low, you could be losing out by keeping your money in a savings account in the bank. Investing in stocks and shares could help you achieve greater returns and assist you in reaching the long-term financial goals you have been thinking about for your retirement or your children's futures.

It is a big step to take for the first time when you think about investments and investing for your future. There are many different options to consider. It can be overwhelming and downright confusing for anyone who has not looked at it before.

Here is a quick guide to what you need to think about before you start and how investments work.

Are you ready to invest?

You should have several things in place before venturing into the world of investments. There is an element of risk involved with any investment, some more than others, so it is worth thinking about how you feel about taking a risk with your cash.

You do not need to be afraid of it, just aware that you need to be prepared for the fact that you could lose some or all of your money depending on the risk you are taking.

You need to consider:

Understanding the risks.

If you have a strong long-term plan and plenty of spare cash to fall back on, the risk element is not so much of a concern, but if you think that you will have sleepless nights if the market is not performing as you would like it to, it is worth going for something with reduced risk.

What do you want to achieve?

Set a clear goal for yourself. Do you just want a regular income or are you looking for a lump sum in the future? This will tell you how much you need to invest and in what time-frame. This will also tell you how much of a risk you should be prepared to take.

If it is a short-term goal (less than five years), you may want to stick to savings as your investment may not return what you need in a short period if they fall in value. If it is a medium-to-long-term goal (five to 10 years-plus), investing is more appropriate. However, you need to think about your age and state of health to make sure that, if a long-term investment falls in value, you still have the means to earn, to build it back up again.

Regular income versus lump sum.

If you are comfortable with risk and know what you want to invest in, a lump sum is the way to go. If you are more cautious and want to see a regular return, regular savings are the way forward.

A lump sum is investing all your money at one time.

This is where you would invest, say, £10,000 on the stock market at once, whether it is in bonds, shares or units in a trust. They are bought at the same price and you can benefit from any price rises straightaway. The downside is that if whatever you have invested in goes down, your money will too. This is where long-term investing can work as it gives the market time to recover. You have to keep a regular eye on the markets.

Regular savings, known as 'pound cost averaging'.

This is where you regularly invest a set amount each month into your chosen shares over a period of time. If the share price goes down one month, you will be able to buy more shares for your money, so by the end of the time period, you could end up with more shares than if you had put in a lump sum. Also, if the share price drops, only the money you have in at that time will be affected rather than the whole lump sum. The downside is, if the share price continues to rise over time, you will not benefit as much as you will not have all of your money invested.

Do you have savings?

Prepare for the unforeseen.

Make sure that your income is protected before you invest. It's worth ensuring that if you could not work for an extended period of time that you and your family will be able to pay the bills.

Getting your priorities straight.

Make a start by matching your income sources against your income needs and then work out which sources will pay for which needs.

If you do not have enough to cover your survival step, there are serious changes that need to be made in order for you to be able to pay your bills.

If you find you only have enough money to pay for survival and safety at this point, you will at least have the comfort of knowing those two critical bases are covered. It is important at this stage that you look at what insurances you have put in place for you and your family and ensure that they are adequate for your needs.

Thinking about the future – what else to consider?

Begin to view your income not as just a way to pay the bills, but as a means to funding a life — the life *you* want.

Many people do not think about a Will, saying that they will not need it for a long time yet, or that they do not have much and it will go straight to their nearest family member anyway. That is not the case and you must ensure that somewhere in writing is what exactly your wishes are in the event of you passing on.

Making a Will ensures that everything is sorted out quickly and efficiently and without argument among family at a most emotional and stressful time. Dying without making a Will (intestate) means that a court relies on a set procedure set up by the State to distribute any assets and it does not consider any wishes of the deceased.

A Will also helps to reduce Inheritance Tax liability in the sense that, if it is looked at early enough, measures can be put into place to move monies and assets in order to reduce the amount that lies above the tax threshold, which in 2016 was £325,000.

Setting up trusts within a Will can be extremely valuable in Estate Planning for a number of different reasons.

When it comes to protecting assets and controlling the distribution of your estate, trusts are essential and advisers can provide a variety of different solutions depending upon your objectives.

Despite changes in legislation, there are still some valuable reasons for establishing trusts in your Will and there are still Inheritance Tax benefits. Having certain assets "ring fenced" in a trust can ensure that your children are not paid outright.

Should a surviving partner become infirm and need to go into long-term care, funds in a trust would not feature in terms of local authority means testing. This is subject to certain criteria.

Often, the solution to a complex situation can be with the use of a trust, which can be created as a stand-alone document that is set up while alive and comes into force immediately or, if written into your Will, upon your death.

Some of the more common trusts found in modern Wills are used for protecting your property after your death. You may wish to leave your property to your children but by using a trust, this will allow you to provide for your spouse or partner for the rest of their life.

Avoiding Inheritance Tax legally can be an accounting or legal minefield but the one guaranteed route, wholly endorsed by the Inland Revenue, is by way of a Discretionary Will Trust, either set up in your lifetime or within your Will to be brought into effect on the first death of a couple.

10 Reasons to make a Will.

- You would have control on what happens to your estate.
- To avoid disagreements on how your assets are divided. Sadly, it is increasingly common for relatives to take court action among themselves, splitting families apart.
- To avoid your family becoming involved in unnecessary costs or delays, which could amount to tens of thousands of pounds.
- You choose who looks after any young children.
- If you were cohabiting without being married, the lack of a Will could mean your partner would have no automatic right to any of your property and could be evicted.
- To ensure there is sufficient money left to comfortably provide for your partner or spouse.
- To prevent your family home being sold to distribute your estate. You can make this position clear and ensure your spouse is not left homeless.
- To avoid your estate paying tax unnecessarily – leaving less to distribute amongst the family.
- To provide protection for your business partners, ensuring there is no forced sale of your business.
- To provide you with peace of mind.

Power of Attorney.

This defines who is responsible for any individual if they become incapable of dealing with their own finances or day-to-day needs, physically or mentally. It provides for the carer to talk to doctors and solicitors with the vulnerable individual knowing that they are being looked after properly and their needs are being dealt with correctly. The mistaken belief is that Power of Attorney is protection for our elders should they get Alzheimer's disease. However, an accident or illness can happen to anyone at any age.

It is never too early to put a Power of Attorney agreement in place... and those who have elderly relatives should talk about this situation while they are capable of discussion it lucidly. If you do not have such an agreement in place, making arrangements can be protracted and heavy costs can be incurred. This can be very unhelpful if you are trying to organise a care home for an elderly relative and you cannot get to their finances to pay for it. I know a friend who took months to get this sorted out for her grandmother who was in hospital in the meantime as she had no one at home. The hospital kept wanting to get her out because they needed the bed, but there was no money to pay anyone to look after her anywhere else.

TAX.

This is a massive area of consideration when making financial decisions. Income tax, Inheritance Tax and Capital Gains Tax must be taken into account. There are several factors to take into consideration.

- Your assets may be gaining value but they are also increasing your Income Tax position.
- Keeping assets in certain places can cause Inheritance Tax issues.
- Cashing in the wrong investments can leave you with Capital Gains Tax to pay.

These are just a few of the areas that clients need to consider in financial planning. An experienced financial planner would be able to work through the implications of all the different areas and make recommendations on the impact this will have on the client.

And here is your seventh of 10 ways to accelerate your wealth –

Number 7:

This is where I can start to lose people. Some can drift off, put the book down and intend to pick it up later, but don't! Stick with it, we are at the good stuff. It can become overwhelming with the number of options or actions you might need to take.

Take a moment to access where you feel you are with your knowledge. Is there a subject you understand more than others? Do you need to consider what subjects might need reading again or researching more? There is always more to learn and you are right where you are meant to be.

12

FINANCIAL CHECK LIST

The Financial Priorities Pyramid can be a lot to take on board if you are at the beginning of your financial journey. We are not all the same and have different needs, it is okay if you have a few things on your to-do list.

Below is a check list to read over with YES or NO answers required:

1. Emergency Funds Position.

Do you have three times the level of regular monthly financial commitments?

2. Pension Position.

Do you have sufficient income in retirement?

3. Estate Planning.

Do you understand your Inheritance Tax position?

Do you have a Will in place?

If yes, and you have children, did you set up guardianship for your children within it?

Do you know if your estate would benefit from a trust?

4. Mortgage Position.

Is your mortgage guaranteed to be repaid before retirement?

Have you had independent advice on this mortgage?

5. Personal and Family Protection Position.

Does your life insurance fully cover the correct mortgage and any debts outstanding?

Does your life insurance extend to cover over and above the mortgage for all other lifestyle costs?

6. Critical Illness Position.

Does your policy fully cover the correct mortgage term and the term of any debts outstanding?

Does your policy cover you for the illnesses you would expect?

Does your insurance extend to cover over and above the mortgage for all other lifestyle costs?

7. Income Protection Position.

Does your income protection position cover at least 50% of your income for long-term illness?

And here is your eighth of 10 ways to accelerate your wealth –

Number 8:

You have answered yes or no to the questions in the check list. Write down all the things you have answered NO to.

Now prioritise your top five.

Work on one at a time, perhaps one week. Do not feel you need to jump in trying to do everything at once, things will get missed and you will get overwhelmed.

Here are some helpful actions for you:

1. Ring your pension provider.
2. Get your insurance policies out and review what you have.
3. Contact a broker to get quotes for any top-ups.
4. Review your mortgage rates as and when they are up for review.
5. Set up an extra bank account for any savings pots.
6. Increase your pension contributions.
7. Contact a solicitor or Will writer to discuss your estate planning.
8. Set up an appointment with an Independent Financial Adviser.

13

THE ECONOMY AND HOW IT AFFECTS INVESTMENT DECISIONS

There is a saying that if China sneezes the United States of America catches a cold. Going back to during 2015 and 2016, China played a massive part in how the stock market performed globally. Below, we discuss how this became the case, what volatility it created and if there are alternatives to investing in the stock market.

In August 2015, China decided to change the way they calculated their exchange rates, causing depreciation in the Yuen and estimated losses of US$5trillion dollars. It is believed that China did this to make exports more competitive and therefore increase their overall economy as their inflation rates were low and they were seeing a decline in spending, including fuel consumption. Together with this, the slowdown in Asia's market would give the USA a chill.

China's stock market, until June 2015, was picking up pace due to new laws allowing funds to invest and firms to offer shares to the public, along with changes in mortgage lending. It was inflating the stock market. This took a downturn when there were concerns over the unsustainable growth. Companies started to freeze their share options causing investors to sell their stock.

Due to the slow economic global growth, oil prices dropped. It was a simple 'supply and demand' issue. Oil is one of the global products that countries such as China need to import and countries such as the USA were over producing to export it. Though China would benefit from this drop in price, their consumers were not demanding it, thus causing a drop in revenue to those who are exporting, so they mass produced even more to make up their margins.

For the first time in seven years, the USA increased their interest rates by 0.25%, as they felt their economy could with-stand the change. There was much talk of this happening in 2016 for the UK also, however the Bank of England needed to be sure it would not reduce inflation and spending due to increasing mortgage payments and loan rates. This change in the USA market did cause the stock market to decrease with the demand and price.

These key areas caused the stock market to be volatile, meaning confidence fluctuated and therefore, so did the prices.

How do all key areas affect the stock market?

Let's discuss what areas could affect the stock market and why. We have mentioned interest rates, inflation and deflation, imports and exports, and foreign markets.

Do you remember your last work party, when everyone was talking about it and how much they were looking forward to it and it caused a buzz in the office? Or do you remember when there was a meeting coming up and everyone was a little worried of what the outcome might be... The stock market is fuelled by these highs and lows. These 'Chinese whispers' of what might be the longer-term outcome of certain facts change by the minute.

If a company launches a new product that is 'cutting edge', this would cause a buzz and people would want to buy those stocks – meaning the prices increase with demand. If companies are not doing so well, so start to sell off their stock, then so might other investors, causing stocks to drop in price.

Inflation is the rate at which the price of goods and services increases. It is the result of several factors, including a rise in the cost of manufacturing, transporting and selling goods. When inflation is at a low rate, the stock market responds with a surge in selling. High inflation causes investors to think that companies may hold back on spending; this causes an across the board decrease in revenue and the higher cost of goods, coupled with the drop in revenue, causes the stock market to drop. Deflation is when the cost of goods drops. While deflation sounds like it should be welcomed by investors, it actually causes a drop in the stock market because investors perceive deflation is the result of a weak economy.

When the economies in foreign countries are down, companies cannot sell as many goods overseas as they used to. This causes a drop in revenue, and that can show up as a drop in the stock market. Foreign stock exchanges also have an effect on the stock market. If foreign exchanges start to fail or experience sharp drops, that kind of activity can cause investors to anticipate a ripple effect, resulting in a drop in the stock exchange.

Therefore, when China changed the way it calculated its exchange rates to improve the cost of exports, this caused a drop on the stock market also. When China changed their laws around how funds could be invested and lending issued to borrowers, it initially caused people to invest more in the stock market. However, this was a fake increase and people realised quickly that it was a temporary boom. Investors and companies jumped out of the markets, freezing their shares and selling them off, causing prices to further drop.

Higher interest rates mean that money becomes more expensive to borrow. To compensate for the higher interest costs, companies may have to cut back spending or lay off workers. Higher interest rates also mean that companies cannot borrow as much as it used to, and this has an adverse effect on business earnings. All of this adds up to a drop in the stock market. Thus, linking back to inflation; the more people spend, the more a business has in revenue and the more their stock prices increase.

So, where does the oil prices fit into all of this?

China, Europe and Japan have slowed their need for oil (fuel) as less people are using cars and companies are not transporting as many goods. The demand has dropped so the price of oil has dropped in an attempt to sell more of it. This is one of the first signs that the economy has slowed, supplying a third of the world's energy resources. Oil is produced by several key countries, with China being one the biggest consumers. The USA started to produce massive levels of oil in recent years due to having a high demand and political reasons with foreign relationships. Oil slumps do not have a direct effect on the stock market but are a key indicator on what is happen in the global economy.

So, you see that the global economy is linked. These changes in the economy change the stock market prices causing peaks and troughs in the value of stocks. This is described as volatility. The measurement of volatility is called 'standard deviation' and it is bench-marked by 'expected return'. If a share price fluctuates between four to five per cent, this would be classed as having low volatility. If the investment fluctuates greatly between from the expected return and has a higher standard deviation this would be classed as being 'volatile' and higher risk. Timing and assessing what might happen is crucial when buying and selling shares. This is known as a 'spread' - the difference between the buying price and selling price. Fund managers would be looking for a share that has standard deviation with a low volatility, providing a good expected return without the risk.

Typically, if you invest in one company's shares, this would be classed as high risk as you are placing all your investment in one area. Diversification is where you spread this risk into not just different funds, as in the stock market or equities, but also other forms of investment that are not reliant on the global economy volatility. These could be cash, fixed-interest securities and property. This would give you a balanced portfolio.

Diversification is measured by correlation between asset classes. Correlation is the relationship between two different types of assets, taking into account performance. This is measured with numbers from +1 to -1, the extent to which assets classes tend to rise and fall together. Fund managers or investors would be looking at the correlation to see if they are cancelling each other out or one is outperforming the other. Another way of diversification in a portfolio is to invest in different industries or different countries: UK, Europe and worldwide.

And here is your ninth of 10 ways to accelerate your wealth –

Number 9:

Do you have any existing investments or pensions? They will be invested into different assets and funds. Do you know how they are invested?

If you have not already, contact the relevant companies and ask them about how the money is invested, what kind of fund is it and the break-down of countries and assets into which the money is invested.

Read more in the next chapter about risk and assets…

14

ETHICAL INVESTING – HOW ETHICAL ARE YOU?

Our world is in crisis.

According to a leaked draft of the upcoming assessment by the UN's leading climate scientists, climate change and biodiversity loss will fundamentally change life on this planet within the next thirty years.

But there is hope. We can still build a better world.

To do this, we need to make significant social and environmental changes. And we need to make them now.

Recycling at home is all well and good, but if we want rapid systemic transformation, we must refocus where the world's money goes. Essentially, we need to get the banks and fund managers behind building back better, stronger, and more responsibly.

Ethical investing has the power to achieve this.

The trouble is that a lot of people have questions and concerns around ethical investing. They want to be sure they can go about it in a way that best serves them and the causes they are passionate about. Given the growing complexity of investment concepts and products catering to this sector, that is no easy task.

What is ethical investing?

Ethical investing is about using your money to do good, or using it to help organisations to do good with it, while you earn.

When choosing ethical investments, firms involved in harmful activities are usually filtered out and companies working hard to positively impact the world are included.

Who is making ethical investments?

A wide variety of investors are using their money to make a difference through moral investment. These include non-governmental organisations (NGOs), religious institutions, private foundations, pension funds and insurers, finance institutions, fund managers, and individual investors.

Some investment specialists believe the increased popularity of ethical investing among individuals is to do with people realising they can incorporate their values and preferences into their investment decisions. However, other experts say that filling your investment portfolio with companies that operate sustainably is simply good risk management.

Either way, the ethical investment market is growing at a staggering pace.

According to Chicago-based investment research firm Morningstar, funds that invest according to environmental, social and governance (ESG) criteria attracted net inflows of £50.2billion globally between April and June 2020.

The UK is the second-largest country in Europe for ethical investing. Sustainable UK assets have grown more than 1,800% from £2.9billion to £56billion since 2003. And, according to the Investment Association, net retail sales into responsible funds averaged more than £1billionn per month in 2020.

Ethical investing has officially hit the mainstream.

That said, in the UK, a high percentage of equity income funds continue to invest in tobacco companies, the oil and gas sector, mining, aerospace, and defence businesses – all problematic industries for ethical investors. You may be surprised to learn that many ESG funds are open to a +/-10% risk of exposure to these areas.

So, to feel comfortable and confident with how your money is working for you and the world, it is essential to decide what your investment priorities will be before committing to a specific investment channel or strategy.

Key Terms.

Below are some of the most common terms used in relation to ethical investing. It is important to understand these as they each have different implications for investments.

ESG.

ESG stands for environmental, social, and governance. Together with more traditional performance measures, it looks at the eco-consciousness, social-consciousness, and operational practices of an organisation that could affect its viability for investors. However, the primary intention of ESG valuations is ultimately to determine financial performance.

Common ESG factors include:

- Environmental: pollution, waste management, carbon emissions, energy usage, animal welfare, etc.
- Social: health and safety regulation, employee relations, child labour, human rights, community engagement, etc.
- Governance: transparency and disclosure, conflicts of interest, board independence, management quality, etc.

SRI.

Socially Responsible Investing looks at ESG investments through an additional layer of ethical guidelines. It actively eliminates or selects investments according to specific negative or positive screens, which could be motivated by religion, personal values, or political beliefs. The aim is for the investor to have a clear conscience while increasing their returns.

Examples of negative SRI screens include:

- Weapon production, addictive substances, terrorism, etc.
- Positive SRI screens include:
- Charitable contributions, community investment schemes, use of renewable energy sources, etc.

Impact Investing.

Having a positive impact on society or the environment is the number one aim of impact investing. This is where an investor would have the opportunity to support a variety of solutions to urgent global social and environmental challenges while also producing financial returns. Impact investing covers areas such as:

- Education, healthcare, sanitation, conservation, agri-tech, clean energy, etc.

An example would be investment into a start-up that is developing a new desalination technology to deliver portable water to people affected by drought.

As stand-alone investments, these can carry higher risk than a diversified trust-based portfolio.

Important Organisations.

Investment firms predominantly use the principles and standards of the following organisations to evaluate the ethics and sustainability of potential investments.

It is important that the trusts and/or companies within your investment portfolio meet these standards and that you understand how your fund manager has used them as a reference point to assess and select investments on your behalf.

PRI.

The Principles for Responsible Investment (PRI) was established as an independent organisation, supported by the United Nations, to promote the incorporation of ESG considerations into all investment decision-making, globally.

More than 2,300 financial institutions, responsible for over USD$80trillion in assets worldwide, are signatories to the PRI's six key principles and voluntarily file regular reports describing their progress in terms of these principles.

- Principle 1: We will incorporate ESG issues into investment analysis and decision-making processes.

- Principle 2: We will be active owners and incorporate ESG issues into our ownership policies and practices.
- Principle 3: We will seek appropriate disclosure on ESG issues by the entities in which we invest.
- Principle 4: We will promote acceptance and implementation of the principles within the investment industry.
- Principle 5: We will work together to enhance our effectiveness in implementing the principles.
- Principle 6: We will each report on our activities and progress towards implementing the principles.

The **PRI** believes that investors are crucial in creating a sustainable global economy that addresses climate change, biodiversity, and human rights challenges. So, it works with its members to encourage tangible and impactful changes aligned with the UN's Sustainable Development Goals.

GIIN

The Global Impact Investing Network (GIIN) promotes the expansion and effectiveness of impact investing around the world.

The organisation creates resources and supports activities, education, and research that help accelerate the development of a coherent impact investing industry. It aims to reduce obstacles to impact investment by providing resources and infrastructure, so more investors can fund positive, impactful solutions to the world's most serious challenges.

One of these resources is **IRIS+**. This is a free, publicly available resource that provides impact measurement and management (IMM) data and comparability, as well as access to practical guidance. It is intended to promote transparency, credibility, and accountability so that decisions around impact investments become easier for everyone.

MSCI

This is an acronym for Morgan Stanley Capital International, a leading investment research firm providing stock indexes, performance analytics, portfolio risk and other tools to institutional investors and hedge funds.

The company's comprehensive ESG ratings measure a firm's resilience to long-term ESG related financial risks. This enables socially conscious investors to filter potential investments to match their values and investment aims.

MSCI's ESG ratings are based on data from financial statements, corporate filings, and third-party sources such as the media, regulators, and governments. It sees a "leader" (rated AAA & AA) as a company leading its industry in ESG risk and opportunity management. Conversely, companies with a mixed ESG track record are rated as "average" (A, BBB, or BB), and a company with high exposure, failure to manage significant ESG risks, and lagging its industry is labelled a "laggard" (with a B or CCC rating).

How ethical Are You?

People often have different views on what makes an investment ethical.

For some investors, it is about ensuring their investments exclude companies involved in potentially damaging activities. For others, it's essential that their money is making a positive impact in specific areas. Finally, some people are less prescriptive but want their investment into a company to promote ethical ideas and environmental and social good within the business.

To align your investments with your values, it is important to understand the levels of ethical policy offered by different types of investment firms.

From an independent financial advisory perspective, there are three levels of ethical investing.

1) Light Touch.

If you want your investments to be environmentally friendly and socially responsible, but you are not at the point where you want complete exclusion and are determined to pick your portfolio apart, then this level of ethical investment is for you.

Investments at this level are primarily reliant on general ESG funds. Sometimes described as "hampers full of sustainable investments", they are a group of stocks from different companies that you can purchase altogether. Compared to purchasing individual stocks, ESG funds help to reduce market risks.

Unlike mutual funds, ETF (exchange-traded funds), and bond funds, ESG funds only include companies that comply with their sustainable and responsible principles. They are usually selected and maintained passively according to each fund's ESG rating. If you are a beginner and want to earn good revenue with a relatively small initial investment, these funds are the ideal option for you.

However, some passively managed funds that claim to involve sustainable or socially conscious investing companies have an even weaker ESG screening process than some mainstream investment funds do. As a result, there is often a 10% or higher risk of exposure to unethical activities such as animal testing or fossil fuel extraction. This depends on the strategy of the investment firm and how they manage their funds.

So, if you are looking for a reliable ESG fund with less likelihood of exposure to unsavoury activities, actively managed funds would be more suitable.

2) **Intermediate.**

This is what we like to call the "in-between" level of ethical investing, where funds are usually selected from model portfolios. This level will suit you if you want your investments to be environmentally friendly and socially responsible, and you have two to three areas you are particular about.

With this approach, you can be sure that certain things are excluded but, more importantly, the emphasis changes here to impact. So, for example, PRI, ESG, and SRI issues are incorporated into analyses, and the investment firm clearly states that they adhere to these standards.

Besides the standards they use, it is also essential to understand the investment firm's strategy. You may, for example, want to exclude companies that have excellent internal ESG policies and do their best to avoid doing harm, but that may not necessarily be doing good externally. Again, you would need to be sure that your investment firm's strategy covers this.

This active approach can be more expensive in some cases, but it is becoming easier to manage because of continuous improvements in technology and regulation. So, the cost of investing in this way is far lower than it used to be.

If this approach is still not enough and there are a lot of activities you would like excluded from your portfolio, or areas of impact you would like to see your investments support, then it is likely you would need to opt for a bespoke ethical investment service.

3) Bespoke.

Specialist ethical investment firms offer tailored investment solutions for clients who are very particular and do not want the chance of any exposure to anything unethical or unsustainable.

Here, a direct fund manager makes a custom selection of companies for you instead of selecting a general ethical fund. They can apply your exclusionary screens to a wide range of investments, including social impact trusts and infrastructure investments.

Also, if they offer tax-efficient portfolio management, they will take your tax planning requirements into account. Bespoke investment services often include first-class custom impact strategies and secure detailed reporting and analysis.

As with any tailored service, this is the most expensive way to invest ethically. It also usually requires a minimum of a £100,000 - £250,000 investment to ensure that the cost of the direct fund manager's services can be covered. However, bespoke ethical investing allows you to rest assured that your investment portfolio adheres to all the exclusions and impact selections you have made, while offering you the highest possibility of excellent returns.

Types of Exclusions.

Common exclusions from ethical funds are companies that have anything to do with alcohol, gambling, tobacco, armaments, pornography, and nuclear power. Additional exclusion criteria beyond these vary from one fund to another.

Some funds exclude a broader range of activities, such as pesticide production or genetic engineering. Others include organisations that profit from controversial activities, as long as no more than 10% of their overall profits come from those activities.

This is why it is essential not to assume that every ethical fund matches your values. Be prepared by stipulating the exclusions you would like your investments to avoid.

Keep in mind that you may not necessarily need to exclude an entire sector for your portfolio to be ethical. For example, by excluding the automotive industry, you might miss out on opportunities to invest in manufacturers working to reduce greenhouse gas emissions or improve road safety standards.

Some popular exclusions are:

Environmental:

- Thermal coal,
- Oil, gas, or coal extraction,
- Oil and gas transition laggards,
- Non-renewable electric usage transition laggards,
- Those in breach of internationally recognised conventions on biodiversity,
- Manufacturers of PVC, ozone-depleting chemicals, and hazardous pesticides.

Socially conscious:

- Human rights violations,
- Poor labour relations,
- Corruption,
- Racism.

Animal welfare:

- Animal testing,
- Intensive farming,
- Abattoir or slaughterhouse operation,
- Producers or retailers of meat, poultry, fish or dairy products.

Banking:

- Exposure to large corporate or Third World debt.

Genetic engineering:

- Patented genes.

Aiming for Impact.

Many ethical investors want to ensure that the funds and/or companies they are investing in go beyond avoiding doing harm and actively work towards having a positive impact on the world.

This is not just about meeting their moral obligations. Data is increasingly showing that investing for impact generates healthy returns and mitigates risk.

When considering the impact, it is helpful to think about SDG-aligned outcomes that enhance investors' portfolios while improving life on our planet. According to the STG framework, areas companies could be working towards are:

1. No Poverty,
2. Zero Hunger,
3. Good Health and Well-being,
4. Quality Education,
5. Gender Equality,
6. Clean Water and Sanitation,
7. Affordable and Clean Energy,
8. Decent Work and Economic Growth,
9. Industry Innovation and Infrastructure,
10. Reduced Inequality,
11. Sustainable Cities and Communities,
12. Responsible Consumption and Production,
13. Climate Action,
14. Life Below Water,
15. Life on Land.

Some investment firms provide impact reports, which help to understand how funds are contributing towards these goals and making a genuine difference. Companies also often publish their individual ESG, SRI, and impact reports on their websites for the public to access freely. Reading and comparing these is an excellent way to understand the positive impact your investment might have.

What's the future of ethical investing?

Investment experts believe the ethical investment industry is going to continue to grow for the foreseeable future. This is largely due to the strong ethical motivations of millennials, who will make up 75% of the workforce by 2025 and are likely to demand that their pension investments follow ethical guidelines.

Also, the UK Government has recently issued the country's first-ever Sovereign Green Bond, announced that it would be the first country in the world to make a Task Force on Climate-related Financial Disclosures (TCFD) fully mandatory across the economy by 2025, and set the target of net zero by 2050. With initiatives like these supporting the green economy, ESG related investments are likely be bolstered even further across numerous sectors.

15

RISK AND ASSETS

An Efficient Frontier
The Power of Diversification

Note: Our bond returns are based on the Merrill Lynch 7-10 Year U.S. Treasuries Index. Our stock returns are based on the total return of the S&P 500 index. Data goes from 1977-2011.

Return - Average of annual returns

Risk - Measured by the standard deviation of annual returns

www.youngresearch.com

This graph above highlights diversification using the theory. This illustrates the highest returns are 100% stocks, however, it also has the highest risk, whereas a package of 50% stocks and 50% bonds reduces the return by just over 1.5% and the risk reduces by a near 8%.

This theory considers the expected values, standard deviations and correlations of assets in the portfolio in order to calculate the portfolios expected return and volatility of a portfolio.

So, if not just equities, where else could you look to invest?

We briefly mentioned cash, fixed-interest securities and property. Let us take a closer look at those.

- Cash is also known as deposit-based investments – these are where the capital does not grow but the capital receives an interest return either monthly or annually. These would start with your typical bank and building society accounts, with online only accounts, or full banking facilities with cheque book, to include deposit accounts. These usually operate with a notice period for withdrawing funds – though this is usually a variable interest rate and is in line with the Bank of England. Fixed interest products usually tie monies into an account for one to five years, providing a slightly higher return but there is limited access to the money without having to pay penalties.
- National Savings products are also 'cash' or deposit-based investments, with a wide range of types of products available.
- Premium Bonds offer a tax-free money prize , and the more you buy the more likely you are to win. Funds can be withdrawn without penalty at any time.
- Income bonds provide a monthly income and can be open from the age of seven or can be purchased for

those younger than seven years old. The bonds can be cashed in at any time without notice or penalty. These are not always available as they are issued in tranches.

- Guaranteed equity bonds provide 100% return of capital at maturity together with potential growth linked to the performance of the FTSE 100 over the term of the bond. Any gains would be subject to capital gains tax.

These kinds of savings are classed as low risk, as the capital will be returned to the investor. The Financial Services Compensation Scheme provides compensation to deposits, although limitations are in place, £85,000 per investor or £170,000 for a joint account.

- Fixed-interest investments, as the title reveals, provide a fixed interest rate and income, often referred to as bonds.
- Amongst these are gilts, known to be a safer way to invest as the State is unlikely to default on payments. Gilts are available to a wide range of investors, so it can be competitive. They can be bought and sold for amounts above or below their face value. They can be short or longer term, up to 15 years. Another benefit is they are being traded on the stock market, sometimes 2% to 3% above market rates. Gilts come in two forms: fixed interest and index linked. With the interest rate fixed, a long-term investment does run the risk of not keeping up with inflation, whereas this would not happen with an index linked product.
- Corporate bonds are not issued by the treasury, but by companies themselves as a way of raising funds. Therefore, they involve greater risk as the company

could default on payments, but they can provide a higher return due to that increased risk. They pay a fixed rate of interest and have a redemption value at the end of the bond period.

Investing in property.

According to the Nationwide House Price Index, published by the Nationwide Building Society, the average price of a house in the UK increased from £59,587 to £189,002 in the 25 years to December 2014. We have seen slumps in the market in recent years, not least in 2008. However, by 2010, the market was level again – and by 2014, we were seeing increases in property values. More recently, house prices have grown 13.4% in 2021, the highest rise since 2004. The question is, when could the bubble burst?

Property in the UK is seen to be a stable investment and some people prefer it as it is something physical to possess, rather than having an asset simply on a piece of paper. Putting residential homes aside, property investing is not as simple as writing a cheque to a fund manager for them to invest for you, unless of course you use a property finder or agent. There are many layers to consider before jumping into a property purchase.

There is often a larger lump sum regarded for a deposit and there could be costs involved to prepare the property for letting, as well as solicitors and mortgage fees. However, investors still see the potential of large returns even over a five-year period, so they feel property is a limited risk with high returns. Typically, an investor would be looking to not only receive a growth return, but also an income return. This is determined by the rental yield.

Rental yield is the total amount of rent received by a tenant minus the running costs (mortgage payments, insurance, repairs and maintenance etc.), divided by the total amount invested to purchase the property (that should include all fees, including tax and legal fees).

One way of investing in property without directly buying a property is by investing in listed property companies on the Stock Exchange, however this could be classed as high risk as you are investing in one particular industry. Via unit trusts or open-ended investment companies that are pooled investments, the investors are buying a share in a portfolio of properties. Often smaller investments can be made and the risk is spread across a range of properties.

To have a diverse portfolio, it is wise to consider ISAs, which are a tax-free range of savings vehicles, consisting of a cash ISA, which is comparable to a deposit savings account, and a stocks and shares ISA, which usually has a maximum total balance per tax year.

The ranges of stocks and shares that can be held are:

1. Shares,
2. Unit trusts and OEICS – equity, bond, cash,
3. Investment trusts,
4. Gilts,
5. Corporate bonds etc. plus many of the products we discussed.

The obvious benefit of investing via an ISA and using your allowance each year is the tax relief. Any interest received is paid gross and is not taxable. Capital gains tax does not apply when disposing of the assets, though losses cannot be offset against it either.

All the other options are subject to tax or CGT in some shape or form. Property rental income is subject to income tax and is run like a business, where some costs can be deducted, such as maintenance of the property. Allowances for mortgage interest was phased out from April 2016. Gains made on the sale of the property would be subject to CGT but annual allowances apply – amounts depend on the relevant tax year.

Apart from open-ended investment companies and gilts, most other investing options are subject to CGT, open ended investment companies are exempt, meaning the funds can grow free of any future tax. However, income tax is payable.

The first set amount of dividend income in each tax year will be tax-free. Sums above that will be taxed at a fixed % for basic-rate taxpayers, a higher rate % for higher-rate taxpayers and higher again for additional-rate taxpayers.

Pensions, of course, should not be forgotten as they have a lifetime allowance far greater than any other investment, around the million-pound mark, but this changes based on the tax year. They also provide an annual allowance to put into the pension each year, again this can change based on what HRMC set out. These are set by the Government and based on policy at the time.

Taking all these factors into consideration, the next element to be considered, is you.

As an investor, what are you looking to achieve?

What are your feelings towards the different levels of risk? And what kind of returns where you hoping for?

Are you more interested in receiving an income now or in the future? Or were you hoping to achieve capital growth longer term?

Did you want to access any monies quickly and how much?

If you were to pop it away, how long would you be comfortable investing the money for?

By assessing your current portfolio position, how diverse is it? How much is in easy access emergency accounts, providing you low returns? Or how much is in volatile funds, giving returns but keeping you awake at night?

Going back to the 'An Efficient Frontier' theory, based on the graph at the start of this chapter, by assessing your portfolio ask yourself, where are you on this chart. Are you 50% bonds and 50% stocks and shares? Are you at different ends of the scale? There is no right or wrong answer in terms of what this 'should' look like, but it should represent your needs as an investor.

For example, if you are very cautious and prepared to take only a small element of risk but you are investing in single investments within a limited industry, then this would meet your investment needs.

Other considerations are age and, therefore, where you are in your life cycle. If you are middle, possibly you would be looking to save and invest and can afford to invest medium to long term, whereas someone closer to retirement is likely to want to protect their capital to ensure there is enough to pay an income into retirement.

Lastly, the investor's personal tax position must be taken into account and maximised wherever possible.

And here is your tenth and final of 10 ways to accelerate your wealth –

Number 10:

At the beginning I asked this question:

Imagine if we could create ***an aligned financial plan for an abundant life.*** What would that look like for you or your family or society as a whole?

What does your aligned financial plan look like?

Bring your family and partner into the conversation and start to piece together your five key next major actions to make the shifts you wish to achieve the desired goals. It is never too late.

These goals will change over time, they will evolve, and as life throws you new challenges, your landscape will change. Keep coming back to this process and keep asking yourself the questions we have posed.

16

SUMMARY.

Dear Reader,

Congratulations for reading all the way to the end. I love to read but I know myself, with family and work commitments, even with best intentions I just do not manage it. Let us recap on the 10 ways to accelerate your wealth:

Number 1:

Understand your money story and how it is showing up in your spending, finances and the ways you are reacting to money.

Number 2:

What does being financially emotionally intelligent mean to you?

Number 3:

What stage of the financial abundance matrix are you in?

NUMBER 4:

What needs to change within your current spending procedure? Where do you need to focus your financial efforts? How can you make those changes?

Number 5:

Give your money a job. Live your life in aligned wealth rather than random and haphazard spending.

Number 6:

Set up at least one wealth pot.

Number 7:

Take a step back -Take a moment to access where you feel you are with your knowledge.

Number 8:

A financial check-list. Write down all the things you have answered NO to.

Number 9:

Do you have any existing investments or pensions? They will be invested into different assets and funds. Do you know how they are invested?

Number 10:

What does your aligned financial plan look like?

I started writing this book with the intention to provide a platform for women to start to understand money wherever they were in their journey. If I have helped one person, it was a success. As I began to realise the task I had taken on, I wanted to achieve more than that and would like to help 5,000 women in the next year. I know the impact that will not only have on them, but their families, along with their children's future, and will create a ripple effect that I will never see.

With all the ideas, education and information out there, it is easy to get overwhelmed. I would just ask that you take at least one action a month and stick with it. Then, take a step back and try another. Bit by bit, you can achieve so much. Procrastination and delaying making decisions will not help you to move forward. Baby steps over the period of a year can result in a giant stride forward.

I would love to hear if you found this book helpful. Please do get in touch and let me know. rebecca@rebeccarobertson.co.uk

Much Love Rebecca

LEAVE A REVIEW ON AMAZON

ABOUT THE AUTHOR

Rebecca Robertson is an award-winning author, TedX speaker, Podcast host and Independent Financial Adviser who is passionate about helping women to gain the confidence to plan their financial future and take control of their finances.

With over 21 years' experience in the financial sector, she has been featured in Forbes Magazine, The Financial Times, BBC Radio and other national publications.

As the Times most vouched for Adviser she is also the winner of:

- Financial Adviser of the Year, Women in Finance Awards.
- Role Model of the Year, Women in Financial Advice Awards.
- Customer Service Winner at Kent Women in Business Awards.

As a straight talking, no fluff, financial adviser who runs a successful six-figure business that also supports other women, Rebecca understands the conflicting priorities women face when it comes to finances and created this planner to help them start their journey to financial freedom.

Contact:

Email:

rebecca@rebeccarobertson.co.uk

Website:

www.rebeccarobertson.co.uk

www.evolutionfinancialplanning.co.uk

Facebook:

Rebecca Robertson - Wealth Creation Coach

Podcast

www.rebeccarobertson.co.uk/podcast

CLIENT TESTIMONIALS

My husband would claim to be in control of our finances but is terribly disorganised. Finding Evolution Financial Planning has been a godsend. We've saved ourselves a good chunk of cash each month, but best of all, I now have the peace of mind that our small children will be provided for should the worst happen. I still have a disorganised husband, but I feel much more in control of things now.

— DEB.

Evolution Financial Planning made it a personal approach. I've never really felt like I could have an honest conversation about what I was trying to do, or what my goals were. Having somebody who was interested in me as a human being trying get on in life was really good experience and I felt like I was listened to and my concerns addressed. Investing in Ethical funds has given me great peace of mind.

— SUE.

Evolution Financial Planning was like a clear choice. It is a down to earth process and very reassuring, I was supported with compassion and focus. I now have clarity about my retirement. I have my business paying me a pension as well as my pot that I have from my marriage. I have values alignment and it feels really good. Just seeing the money going straight into my pension, knowing that I have a pot, an investment pot that I can then choose to top that up with, I've got clarity about when to take more money out of the business, when to invest more, you know, I can sort of see all the things lining up. I know I'm in charge of my money, but more so that my money is in alignment with my life.

— Lisa.

Rebecca looked at my finances and recommended a solution to give us more disposable income but still paying off our mortgage. She made everything clear and the process was quick and painless. And unlike many financial advisers, you can easily get hold of her. She always calls you back. I have recommended Rebecca to friends. – Jane.

Rebecca was always up to date with my needs and my family needs. She was very friendly and offered us advice based on my needs. Evolution Financial Planning stood out for me because they did not come across as scary or too intimidating. They were friendly and relaxed. The customer service was brilliant and was always ready to help. – Lorna.

I have had financial advisor for a number of years, and I just didn't really feel connected to my finances, they didn't feel very passionate about what they did. I found Evolution Financial Planning and I was really impressed with Rebecca's backstory with her passion for life and her passion for your finance and business. I just feel much more engaged with my finances.

— KEITH AND SHARON.

"The reason why I've been so financially successful is my focus has never, for one minute, been on money."

— *OPRAH WINFREY.*

REFERENCES

Introduction

1. scottishwidows.co.uk/about_us/media_centre/reports/women-retirement-report/
2. unbiased.co.uk/news/financial-adviser/be-a-woman-with-a-financial-plan
3. fidelity-women-report.pdf (eumultisiteprod-live b03cec4375574452b61bd-c4e94e331c7-16cd684.s3-eu-west-1.amazonaws.com)
4. cebr.com

1. Why women behave differently with money to men

1. theguardian.com/business/2005/apr/22/money.genderissues

Printed in Great Britain
by Amazon